Praise for *A Teachable Faith*

"Encourages all readers to believe that God has a purpose for them and that He is walking with them even through life's trials."
— *Christian Retailing*

"With refreshing honesty Jennifer reminds all of us that God can use everything from a shattered spirit to a stubbed toe in order to teach us and change our hearts. Her spiritual growth since 9/11 is astounding! Regardless of where you are in your walk with the Lord, you will benefit immensely from reading *A Teachable Faith*."
— *Georgia Shaffer, psychologist, author of*
A Gift of Mourning Glories: Restoring Your Life after Loss,
and producer of the syndicated radio feature
"The Mourning Glory Minute."

"A personal relationship with Christ changes our view of everything in life and makes ordinary, everyday circumstances a spiritual object lesson taught by God's Holy Spirit. Jennifer has shared with us her exciting journey of growing in Christ. May the lessons she has taken to heart, reach our hearts as well."
— *Bestselling author Janette Oke*

"As the twin towers fell, I stood numbed by the horror of what I was seeing. Every time I pass through airport security on my frequent trips, I am reminded of the horrendous event that changed our lives. The news of this terrible act of hate reached deep into the Amazon jungle where the people live, who years ago speared my father and four friends. Like us, those families in the jungle ask, why? In this book, Jennifer answers that question. Jennifer's life was devastated by September 11. If she dares to suggest that God had a purpose for what happened in her life, then we should listen. If she can find hope in her circumstances, then we can find hope in ours. The question is not — will tragedy come into our lives? The question is — where will we find peace, hope, and the will to go on when it does?"

— *Steve Saint, author of* End of the Spear,
son of missionary Nate Saint

A Teachable
Faith

A Teachable Faith

Learning from God in Everyday Life

Jennifer Sands

A 9/11 widow's continuing journey

A Teachable Faith: Learning from God in Everyday Life
by Jennifer Sands

FIRST EDITION

The Olive Press, an imprint of Peak Writing, LLC, P.O. Box 14196, Savannah, Ga. 31416

Photo of cross and author portrait on cover: Michael Angelo, Peskin Studio.
Photo of author at Sea of Galilee and Jerusalem: Mike Stanislawski.

Feedback to the author: jennifer@jennifersands.com or visit www.jennifersands.com

For information regarding discounts for bulk purchases, please contact specialsales@theolivepress.net.

Cover and interior design by Pneuma Books, LLC
For more information, visit www.pneumabooks.com

Printed in the United States of America
12 11 10 09 08 07 06   06 05 04 03 02

Publisher's Cataloging-In-Publication Data
(Prepared by The Donohue Group, Inc.)

Sands, Jennifer, 1964-
 A teachable faith : learning from God in everyday life / Jennifer Sands.

 p. : ill. ; cm.
 ISBN-13:978-0-9767961-1-4
 ISBN-10: 0-9767961-1-2
 LCCN: 2005929064

1. Sands, Jennifer, 1964- 2. Spiritual life--Christianity. 3. Spiritual healing. 4. September 11 Terrorist Attacks, 2001--Religious aspects--Christianity. I. Title.

BV4501.3 .S36 2005
248.4   2005929004

The
Olive Press

Mission Statement

Our mission is to give a voice to Christian leaders who have dedicated their lives to bringing God's anointed word and the message of salvation through Christ to others. Every day, men and women all over the world speak to groups with powerful words about the Gospel's life-giving message. The Olive Press exists to record their words in books and other published materials that extend their messages to a broader audience. We pray that this book will speak as deeply and meaningfully to you as it has to us.

*This book has been written in memory and honor of
my husband and soul mate Jim Sands —
Thank you for always making me so happy, hon…
Je T'Aime beaucoup all the days of my life.*

*This book — and every facet of my life — is dedicated
to my Lord and Savior Jesus Christ — I will never forget
the sacrifice You made for me and the love
with which You made it…
and I will never stop trying to show You how grateful I am.*

Contents

Foreword

It was an event like few others in the course of our lives — we will never forget where we were, what we felt, and how we found out. For a variety of reasons, the events of September 11, 2001, impacted each one of us. The memories of that day are forever seared upon our consciousness — or should be — lest we forget the lessons we've learned.

Having grown up in the metropolitan area of New York City, having been to the top of the World Trade Center towers numerous times, having loved the city and the unique spirit of the people, and still having family and friends living and working there made the horrific loss of life and the world-changing events of 9/11 painfully real and still leaves my heart raw to the subject.

In her first book, *A Tempered Faith*, Jennifer Sands expressed what, I believe, many individuals throughout our country may have felt, including her initial reaction of anger toward God. Jennifer's candor in expressing herself regarding the loss of her husband, Jim Sands, Jr., in Tower One, touches each one of us in a most realistic way. Yet, Jennifer doesn't leave us with only the horror and confusion of that day; she leaves us with hope and points us, gradually and gently, to the truth of Jeremiah 29:11 – 14.

> *"For I know the plans I have for you,"* declares the
> LORD, *"plans to prosper you and not to harm you,*

plans to give you hope and a future. Then you will call upon me and come and pray to me, and I will listen to you. You will seek me and find me when you seek me with all your heart. I will be found by you," declares the LORD *(*NIV*).*

I appreciate apologetics, which means I value evidence. *A Teachable Faith* is evidence of a changed heart and life and proof of what happens when you realize that true Christianity cannot be reduced to a set of moral constructs, or a simple identification, or something you practice only on Sunday mornings. It is what happens to a submitted, albeit broken, heart that is fully committed to the Lord Jesus Christ.

God loves you so much that He is willing to allow certain circumstances in your life — even unimaginable ones — in order to draw you into a vibrant relationship with Himself. But as you read this book, I believe you will be encouraged in the reality that God can use you for His glory and use your most painful experiences for a greater, indeed higher, purpose.

Thank you, Jennifer, for sharing your heart and love for Christ with us, for sharing your very personal journey to the cross, and for expressing what many readers may have felt but were unable to articulate. Bless your heart, Jennifer, as you continue to grow in your relationship with our great God and our Savior, Jesus Christ. Your sister and servant in Christ,

— Judy Salisbury, author of *A Christian Woman's Guide to Reasons for Faith: Understanding Why You Believe* and President of Logos Presentation

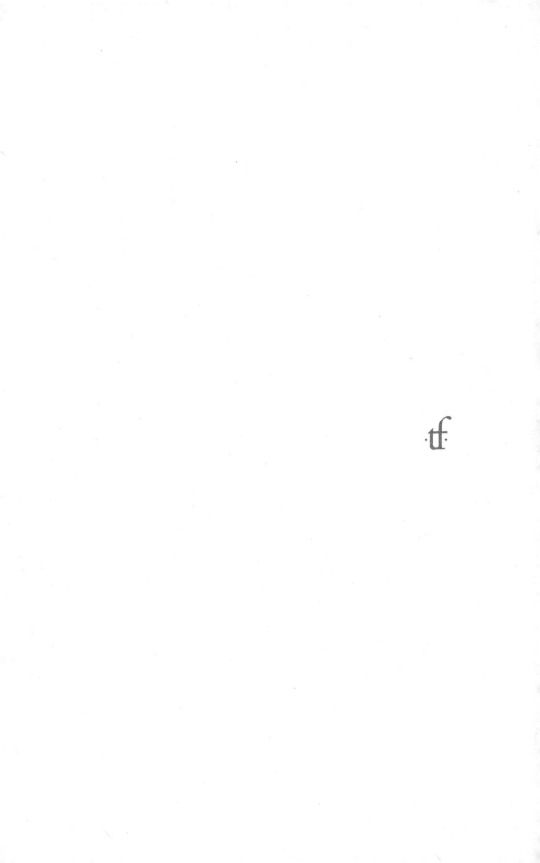

I will instruct you and teach you in the way you should go. I will counsel you and watch over you.

~Psalm 32:8 (NIV)

Preface

I was married for five years to the man of my dreams, Jim Sands. We had a healthy marriage and a promising future. We were successful professionals — I am a pharmacist, and Jim was a computer software engineer. We were avid scuba divers — training to become dive instructors — and Jim had a talented passion for underwater photography. We had hopes and plans and dreams for our lives; we were madly in love, and we were inseparable.

At 6:00 A.M. on September 11, 2001, Jim kissed me good-bye. He said, "I love you," and left for his office on the 103rd floor of Tower One of the World Trade Center. Then I did something that I had done every morning when Jim left for work: I prayed for God to keep Jim safe.

Jim never returned home.

In the personal aftermath of the 9/11 terrorist attacks, despair took me to dark places and pain consumed my life. Since my prayers hadn't been answered the way I wanted them to be answered, my faith was shaken. And I directed all my bitterness and anger straight at God. I soon found myself at a crossroads of faith and was forced to make a choice. Remain bitter at God and the world? Or pick myself up off the ground, take a deep breath, and move onward?

Eventually I realized that being mad at God was proof that I still believed He existed. Since I've never been the type to hold a grudge against anyone, I chose to wave a white flag at the Creator of the universe. *I don't know what you're doing in my life, Lord. I'm not happy about it one bit, but I trust You know what you're doing.* I decided to surrender and submit myself completely to God's will. I put my life and my future in His hands... and peace finally came.

Today, I can look back and see all the ways that God responded to my anger and intervened in my life. He sent in the troops — family, friends, neighbors, even complete strangers. He also blessed me with some amazing tributes to Jim, which gave me something positive to focus on in the midst of such loss. When I stopped challenging God to show Himself, He made Himself known to me. When I stopped flailing my arms in the stormy waters, I began to float peacefully. That's what God promised would happen, and it did.

This book is a companion to *A Tempered Faith*, which I wrote during the time of my spiritual transition. *A Tempered Faith* is the story of the first year of my life after 9/11 and my personal journey toward a greater understanding of being a Christian. *A Teachable Faith* is the report of what God has accomplished in my life since that time and in my ongoing walk with Him.

Perhaps you are reading this book simply because you read *A Tempered Faith*, and you're just curious to know what I've been up to. Maybe, like me, you want to learn more about God. Or perhaps you are reading this book because you're dealing with difficulties in your life and you want to see how I've dealt with mine. Whatever the case, I hope you will benefit from the lessons I have learned and the experiences I share in this book. I hope you will discover (if you have not already) that, by turning to Christ, we can find joy in the midst of our challenging circumstances. May we never lose sight of the One who knows more

xx

about pain and suffering than any of us can fathom. May we always focus on the One who longs to win our heart and bring us through our journey. And no matter how deep the water gets, may our faith always remain strong and... teachable.

tf

For the word of God is living and active. Sharper than any double-edged sword, it penetrates even to dividing soul and spirit, joints and marrow; it judges the thoughts and attitudes of the heart.

~Hebrews 4:12 (NIV)

Required
Reading

1

I will never forget the first time I saw a Scripture verse and it actually meant something to me... when God spoke to me through His Word, and I heard Him loud and clear. As usual, His timing was perfect.

It was a few months after September 11, 2001, during the holiday season. I was alone in the mall, shopping for the few Christmas presents that I would buy that year. At that time in my life, being in the mall was unbearably painful. Shopping was agonizing. Everywhere I turned, I was blasted by reminders of Jim: his favorite clothing stores, Structure and The Gap... the kiosk where he had just bought his new cell phone... Mrs. Field's cookies, which he could never resist... Lenscrafters, a frequent stop because his eyeglasses always needed some kind of adjustment. I was only in the mall for an hour, but it was excruciating, and I couldn't wait to leave.

On my way out, there was no escaping the Salvation Army guy. A large group of people was ahead of me, and the exit became congested as they all fumbled for change. I let out a heavy, aggravated sigh. *Get me out of here. I hate Christmas. I hate my life. I hate the world. I just want to go home and cry for the rest of the day.*

I reached into my pocket for the car keys and discovered a

dollar bill I had stuffed in there a few days before. The crowd in front of me finally cleared out, and I put my dollar bill into the distinctive red donation can. The Salvation Army man smiled and thanked me. I grinned back, instinctively, and he handed me the classic red flower and a small card. I clutched them both in my fist along with my keys and made a mad dash for my car.

The emotional shopping experience and the aching emptiness of the holiday season were too much to bear. I remember walking through the parking lot holding my breath and looking down at the ground so the other shoppers couldn't see the strain on my face as I tried not to explode into tears. *Don't lose it. Don't lose it. Hold it in just one more minute, almost there.* I finally reached my car, struggled with the keys that were now tangled with the red flower, got in, slammed the door, and took a deep breath. I desperately needed a distraction from the pain. I looked down at the small card that the Salvation Army man had given me. On it was a picture of the American flag, a silhouette of the towers bearing the words "9-11-01...We Will Not Forget You," and this Scripture verse:

> *"For I know the plans I have for you... plans to give you hope and a future"* (*Jeremiah* 29:11).

It was the first time in my life — ever — that I had taken notice of a Bible verse. Sure, I had seen Bible verses before... but I never paid attention to them. This time was different. This time I actually felt like I had a dialogue going with God. This time He broke the silence and spoke to me — through a little piece of cardboard with some powerful stuff written on it. His words — so unexpected — were His response to my despair. They went straight to the very core of my soul and planted themselves there.

This realization — that God Himself had just spoken to me — became the drop of water that broke the dam. I sat in my car, looking at the Salvation Army card and crying until my tear ducts once again ran dry. I knew God was there beside me. He heard every sob, saw every tear.

I keep that Salvation Army card in my wallet to this day.

Because of that verse, I actually opened the Bible and started reading it. At that time, my post-9/11 anger and bitterness were beginning to cool off. Family and friends continually offered spiritual support, but I was not always receptive to it. That Scripture verse changed things. Funny how God knows *exactly* when you're ready to hear Him. He knows when you've hit bottom. He knows when you're so desperate you'll try anything to find answers — even read a Book that you've never had any interest or desire to open before...

Now I can't put it down.

ᛏ

Many are the plans in a man's heart, but it is the LORD's purpose that prevails.
~Proverbs 19:21 (NIV)

Taking
Notes

2

Over the course of the next year, God used many people to help me overcome my anger and turn it into a deep love and adoration for Him. I continued to read the Bible, although my lack of Scriptural foundation and a deficient knowledge of its history made it hard for me to understand what I was reading. Before September 11th, the extent of my Biblical understanding was this: There undoubtedly is a God and He sent His Son Jesus Christ to live here, to die for our sins, and to rise again. And somewhere in there was the Holy Spirit, but I was never quite sure where He fit in.

I never took an interest or the time or the effort to move closer to God — I always thought I was as close as I needed to be. I take full responsibility for not pursuing that relationship and for the lack of value that I placed on Jesus' sacrifice for us. Two years after the tragedy, I was still attending the same Catholic church I had been attending for fifteen years. I realized that I was severely deficient in my knowledge of the Bible, so I began reading it on a regular basis. I truly wanted to get closer to God, but I also had no intention of leaving my own church to accomplish that.

Then came *A Tempered Faith*. There are remnants of that spiritual immaturity within its pages, but I believe that this is part of the beauty of watching a person's journey unfold. We cannot appreciate the progression of someone's faith unless we see where the journey began — spiritual ignorance and all.

With the release of *A Tempered Faith* in September of 2003, I was asked to give my testimony at several churches. I had never in my life spoken in front of an audience, so I needed a crash course in public speaking. I received a great deal of help from my sister Maria and her husband Tom, who not only coached me on speaking but also suggested that I visit their church — a Baptist church they have attended for thirty years — for a Sunday morning service. They mentioned that their pastor has tremendous experience as an eloquent speaker both locally and nationally. (Their unspoken goal, of course, was for me to expand my spiritual limits with the hope that I would enjoy the service enough to return again.) I thought to myself, *Hey, that's a good idea. I'll check out the pastor's body language. I'll watch to see how often he makes eye contact with the congregation. I'll see how often he looks down at his notes. I'll listen for the inflection in his voice. Here's a guy who knows how to speak effectively — I'll just follow his example.*

So I joined Maria and Tom in their church one Sunday morning in the summer of 2003. My only intention was to take notes on Speaking Etiquette 101... but God had another plan.

I found out later that Pastor G. Richard Fisher prepares his sermons months in advance, and he had no way of knowing that I would be in attendance that Sunday. As Pastor Fisher began to give his message, I soon found myself unable to focus on his body language, expressions, and inflection. I didn't care how he looked and acted up there. All I heard were his words, and they were like a laser beam that shot directly into my heart. His message that day was about suffering and the trials of life.

And the Scripture passage that he centered on for his sermon? Jeremiah 29:11.

6

By the time the service was over, I knew without a shadow of a doubt that I was exactly where I belonged. I had found my new church family. As Maria and Tom's sister, the church congregation had continually lifted me up in prayer after 9/11; they had been praying for my peace, for my healing, for my salvation, and for God to use this tragedy to bring me closer to Him. They began to see the fruit of their prayers that day.

I wasn't the only member of the family for whom they diligently prayed. My nephew Brian (Maria and Tom's younger son) was a paradigm of the prodigal son. He grew up in a strong Christian family, but he took a moral detour after high school and traveled a dark and vile road on his way to perdition. While the church was praying for me after 9/11, they were also praying for Brian's repentance. Soon after I began attending their church, Brian admitted that his life was a total mess and that Jesus was the only One who could save him from self-destruction. He returned to Christ with more conviction than anyone could have hoped for. Brian and I were baptized together in our church on the same day: October 5, 2003. We both came from the murky depths of the Black Hole — under very different circumstances — but we were both rescued by the grace of God's hands.

Through the emotional and spiritual support of my entire family and many friends, the teaching and study of God's Word, the guidance of Pastor Fisher, and the strong fellowship of the congregation, I have been brought to a new level of faith. I've attended countless Sunday morning and evening church services, Bible studies, and prayer groups at my new church since that day, but I have yet to pay attention to Pastor Fisher's body language or his speaking skills. His strong, Biblically-centered messages always have that same profound effect on me — they come through loud and clear, and nothing else is important.

I know what it is to be in need, and I know what it is to have plenty. I have learned the secret of being content in any and every situation, whether well fed or hungry, whether living in plenty or in want.
~Philippians 4:12 (NIV)

The Cafeteria

3

I love variety. Give me a sampler platter at a restaurant and I'm in my glory. I'm also very particular. I like what I like, and that's all there is to it. Jim used to say that listening to me order at a restaurant provided his entertainment for the evening. He insisted that I must be the joke of the kitchen staff. Here's how Jim would imitate me:

> Yes, I'd like to start with the French onion soup. But hold the onions — just bring the cheese, the bread, and the broth. For my entrée, I'd like the chicken special, but I'd like Marsala sauce instead of garlic and butter — and stuffed with Fontina cheese, instead of Swiss. I'll skip the asparagus. Can I have extra roasted potatoes instead? Oh, and an iced tea, with no ice, unsweetened, and three lemons.

Wouldn't it be nice if the choices in our lives were as easy as ordering from the menu in a restaurant? Sure, sometimes they are. And wouldn't it be great if we could order only the good stuff and ask the server to hold the rest? Sure, sometimes we can. But other times, we aren't given any choice in the matter whatsoever.

9

Excuse me, waitress. There seems to be a mistake here. I ordered the daily special. You know, Happily Ever After with a side of Joy and Good Health? But instead, you've brought me the combination platter of Heartaches, Disappointments, and Suffering. My plate is overflowing, and I didn't even order it!

Boy, does *that* reaction sound familiar to me. No, we didn't order the plateful of burdens. But the Master Chef has determined that *this* is the meal that will nourish us. As difficult as it is to swallow, this is the meal that will make us stronger, and it will help us to grow closer to Him. It may taste like brussel sprouts, but it's good for us.

How often do I fixate on my plateful of burdens instead of determining what it is that God is trying to teach me from it? Only when I discipline my thoughts to focus on God's will — instead of my ordeal — do I find inner peace. And how often do I run to God as the last resort — instead of the first step — in dealing with a problem? I admit it. I'm guilty of Spiritual Negligence in the First Degree. I tend to assume that I'm big enough to handle problems all by myself, so I decline the free consultations He offers me. I forget that He knows the situation better than I do — He knows me better than I do — and He is much more capable of handling it than I am. After all, He's God. I'm not.

There are so many choices in life, yet there are just as many circumstances that we have absolutely no control over. We cannot control the weather; we cannot choose our birth parents; we cannot stop time; we cannot decide when our hair will turn gray. I did not choose to become a widow on September 11, 2001. But the biggest, the most crucial, the most vital decision in the menu of our lives is where we spend eternity. And that choice is ours.

All discipline for the moment seems not to be joyful, but sorrowful; yet to those who have been trained by it, afterwards it yields the peaceful fruit of righteousness.

~Hebrews 12:11 (NASB)

Teacher's
Pet

4

At a neighbor's barbeque recently, I complimented him on how well his three-year-old yellow lab, Zeke, was behaving in spite of the commotion of the party, the splashing of the pool, and the tempting smell of steaks and burgers on the grill. Joe proudly began to show me just how obedient his dog truly is. Zeke patiently sat at his owner's feet while Joe held a juicy, half-eaten hamburger in his outstretched arm above Zeke's head. Zeke panted and salivated as Joe gave firm commands to his dog, "Noooooooo. Not yet. No."

I looked at Zeke and realized the secret of the trick. Zeke was not looking at the hamburger. His eyes were fixed on his master. Zeke was trained to trust Joe, and no matter how great the temptation, Zeke's training taught him to stay focused on his owner. After Zeke proved his obedience for what seemed like an eternity to me, Joe finally gave him the hamburger. Zeke happily trotted off to devour his reward.

God surely has a sense of humor; only He would send a dog to teach me a lesson. The night before the barbecue, I had been laying in bed worrying about what I was going to wear to an up-coming speaking engagement since nothing in my closet seems to fit me anymore. I worried about the prediction of heavy rain on

13

the day of the event, since I'd be driving a long distance in unfamiliar territory. I worried about every possible thing that could go wrong during my program. But after watching Zeke's impressive display of obedience, I knew exactly where my focus must be — on God, my Master, not on the temptations in my life.

In my pre-9/11 days, I used to think that *temptations* only referred to the thought of eating hot fudge sundaes while you're on Weight Watchers. When I first began to read the Bible after 9/11, I still misunderstood the word. I thought *temptations* were limited to immoral thoughts, words, and actions. So I presumed that I was safeguarded against temptation simply because things like alcohol, drugs, gambling, promiscuity, and profanity are simply not a part of my lifestyle.

But then I learned that temptations come in other forms — like worry, anxiety, fear, uncertainty, and doubt. By worrying about things we cannot control, we doubt the One who really *is* in control. By allowing anxiety to consume our thoughts, we fail to trust God and the outcome of His plan. In the course of one day, I am constantly tempted by these emotions — they threaten to block the connection between me and God. And that's far more dangerous than a thousand tempting hot fudge sundaes.

As I watched Zeke, I saw God's creative illustration of how we must train ourselves to trust and obey Him, our own Master, even in the midst of temptation. Zeke waited patiently for his prize, and he eventually received it. Does that mean that if we wait long enough, we will always get what we desire? Nope. We will get what God desires, which may or may not be our own wishes. If Joe knew that hamburger was contaminated with E. coli, he would have kept Zeke's best interest in mind and never allowed the dog to eat it. Of course, Zeke would not have understood *why* he wasn't receiving the one thing he so patiently

14

waited for... and that is where trust and discipline become critical in our walk with the Lord.

In my adolescent years, I resented having strict parents. Back then, their rules seemed so unreasonable and downright embarrassing. I wasn't allowed to ride my bike on the highway. I had to finish my homework and practice the piano before I was allowed to join friends. I definitely had the earliest curfew in town. But because of my conservative upbringing and their virtuous example, I can proudly say this: Thank you, Mom and Dad, for not letting me stay out all night. Thank you for wanting to know who I was spending my time with. Thank you for saying "no" when you needed to protect me... even though I couldn't understand your answer until now.

In the same way, God acknowledges our requests in one of three ways: yes, no, or wait. The yes and no answers are easy to recognize — we may or may not like them, but they're clear and concrete.

It's the "wait" answers that become the real test of patience. *Wait* can eventually turn into a yes or a no, but it's left pending. Jim often joked with me about my intolerance for anything that remained open-ended. I would flip out when an episode of *West Wing* or *ER* ended as an unexpected cliffhanger. I became annoyed if plans with friends or relatives were not confirmed a week in advance. Waiting for the results of blood work has been known to send me into a funk. Of course, I never knew the frustration and pain of waiting more than I did on September 11th.

Elisabeth Elliot, whose husband Jim Elliot was one of five missionaries killed by the Auca Indian tribe of Ecuador in 1956, says it this way in her book, *A Lamp for My Feet*:

> *Faith is the willingness to receive whatever He wants to give or the willingness not to have what*

He does not want to give. Furthermore, faith does not insist upon an explanation. It is enough to know that the Father loves us and gives us only what we are meant to have.

One of the greatest challenges in my walk with the Lord — and I haven't perfected it yet — is keeping my eyes fixed on my Master and not being distracted by the temptations around me. If Zeke didn't get that burger, I have no doubt he would have remained just as loyal to Joe. Dogs love and trust their masters unconditionally, and I needed to learn to love and trust God unconditionally. I needed to align my desires with God's desires. It's my stubborn Sicilian nature to want what I want and to be upset when I don't get it. Conforming to God's plans for my life was a difficult exercise, but the results have far exceeded the effort. I used to believe that everything in life would be so much simpler if the world just did things my way. Now I have learned that my life has been made simple — by doing things God's way.

The wolf will live with the lamb, the leopard will lie down with the goat, the calf and the lion and the yearling together; and a little child will lead them.

~Isaiah 11:6 (NIV)

Elementary School

5

In November of 2000, when my niece Tarah was in second grade, I helped her study for a spelling test. I would say the word, and she would have to spell it. But as I quizzed her, I came to a word that I could not pronounce. I didn't even know what it meant. I thought I was a fairly intelligent person, but I had to admit my ignorance. I confessed, "Tarah, I do *not* know what this word is, and I can't even say it."

She glanced over my shoulder at the workbook and quite matter-of-factly said, "Oh, Leviticus. L-E-V-I-T-I-C-U-S."

I shook my head in disbelief and said, "*What* does... luh...vit... ick... us mean?"

She giggled and rolled her eyes and gave me that silly girl look. "It's the third book in the Old Testament."

"Oh."

Needless to say, I was rather humbled at that moment — and still clueless.

Tarah is my brother Anthony's daughter. She's now thirteen — going on thirty — and she's an absolute delight. I realize I'm not an objective source, so here's my blatantly biased opinion: She's incredibly smart. While her peers read *Teen Beat* magazine, Tarah studies floor plans in *Architectural Digest*. And she's downright adorable — especially when she dresses up in Aunt Jennifer's circa 1981 hot-pink prom gown. Tarah has been raised in a strong, Christian environment, and she's been quite an influence on me.

About a week after the 9/11 attacks, Tarah was at my house — along with many others — and I was wandering around aimlessly in the pit of despair. I do not recall many details from those days since my mind was a blurred mix of painful emotions and way too much Xanax. But I do remember a kind gesture from my precious niece who had just lost her Uncle Jim in the worst terrorist attack in our country's history.

Tarah asked me if we could go to a quiet place, because there was something she wanted to read to me. In my state of grief, all I wanted to do was pull the covers over my head and not talk to anyone, but I can't say no to those big brown eyes. So I agreed. We sat alone at the top of the staircase, and Tarah opened her Bible and began to read several different verses. I half-listened patiently and politely as she tried to comfort me.

She was only nine years old — yet she was reading articulately from the Word of God. I was thirty-seven years old, and I had no familiarity with Scripture whatsoever — nor did I care to hear it. I cannot recall which verses she read, and I was not in a frame of mind to retain them anyway. But I recently attended a Bible study and came across one of them — from Psalm 42. I immediately recognized it as one that Tarah had read to me on that day, and my mind flashed back to the sound of that sweet little voice reciting it three years before: "Why are you so downcast O my soul? Why so disturbed within me? Put your hope in God, for I will yet praise Him, for the help of His presence" (Psalm 42:5, NIV).

God knew way back then that one little passage from Psalm 42 had been deeply embedded into my conscience, and that three years later, something would trigger its release. He knew Tarah's efforts would not be in vain.

Today, my role has been reversed as *I'm* the one often using Scripture to comfort a downcast soul. And though that person's heart may be hardened just like mine was, I know the mighty power of the Word and the endurance of that planted seed. And perhaps that person will one day use Scripture to comfort someone else... and so on... and so on... many links in a chain of God's love, all because a little girl wanted to comfort her grieving aunt. God's classroom has no age or skill requirements. Sometimes the students are teachers and the teachers are students... but we all learn from Him.

tf

For God has not given us a spirit of fear, but of power and of love and of a sound mind.

~2 Timothy 1:7 (NIV)

School
Supplies

6

On April 16, 1991,
I met two friends for a late-night dinner at a local restaurant. We
were all retail pharmacists; we had all worked until closing and
we were hungry and grouchy and needed to vent the aggrava-
tions of the day. It was close to midnight when I left alone, and
as I was approaching my car in the dark parking lot, I was as-
saulted by a man who threw me to the ground. We played tug of
war with my purse, but he won... and he escaped with my purse
in a getaway car. I was fine, though very shaken up and upset
over the lost contents of my wallet. Although there's no guaran-
tee of safety, the incident would likely not have happened if I had
taken better security precautions.

Four years later on May 27, 1995, in the same spot of the
same parking lot of the same restaurant, I met Jim Sands for the
very first time. Less than a year later, we were married. And
every May 27th thereafter, we would go back to our meeting spot
and enjoy a celebratory lunch. For a long time, I referred to that
parking lot as "the place where the *worst* thing and the *best* thing
in my life happened."

Effective September 11, 2001, that statement was no longer
valid.

Did we do everything in our power to prevent the terrorist

attacks on September 11th? Most likely, no. Did we learn from our mistakes, and are we doing everything in our power to prevent it from happening again? Hopefully, yes.

Is it possible to completely prevent crime and terrorist attacks from occurring? Unfortunately, no. There will always be evil forces in this world to contend with — it's called *sin*. It's been going on since the beginning of time; it's why Jesus was sent here.

The apostle Paul said, "Do not be overcome by evil, but overcome evil with good" (Romans 12:21, NIV). Well that's not always easy, Paul. I have difficult and challenging days to contend with. There's only one of me, and I'm only five feet tall. How am I supposed to overcome evil?

I used to think the word *evil* only referred to horrible, wicked things like murder and terrorism or people like Charles Manson or characters like Darth Vader. But evil encompasses much more than that — it is every negative force that we have to battle against every day, like those *temptations* I learned about. Evil is anger, bitterness, fear, disobedience, doubt, idolatry, unforgiveness, deceit, the list goes on… they're all evil in God's eyes because these thoughts and actions didn't come from Him.

Apparently the Ephesians had their own difficulties with overcoming evil, so Paul gave them some good advice. He encouraged them to put on the full armor of God: The belt of truth, the breastplate of righteousness, the shoes of the gospel of peace, the shield of faith, the helmet of salvation, and the sword of the Spirit, which is the Bible (Ephesians 6:13–17). Wow, that's one powerful uniform, and it even comes in petite sizes.

I planned to meet a friend whom I hadn't seen for years at a local coffee shop. She had recently lost her husband to a terminal illness. When we arrived, we discovered that it was "psychic night" at the shop. My friend said, "Hey! Maybe the psychic can tell us where our husbands are!"

I put on the belt of truth, thought about Jesus when He said, "*I am* the Way and the Truth and the Life. *No one* comes to the Father except through Me" (John 14:6, NIV) [emphasis mine], and explained to her why we won't find answers through a psychic. Then I told her about the One in Whom we can find the answers, and I suggested that we go out for ice cream instead. That was the day we discovered Vienna Mocha Chunk at Friendly's — and we haven't stopped talking about it since.

Another friend of mine — who is also a Christian author and speaker — recently spoke at a large conference. After the event, she received her honorarium in the mail — the amount of the check was twice as much as the speaking fee they had agreed upon. We talked about whether or not she should make them aware of it, and the evil one was messing with our heads.

"I could really use the money," she said.

"Maybe they thought you were worth it, and this is a bonus," I said.

"They probably won't even notice the mistake," we both said. But after we prayed about it, we put on the breastplate of righteousness. We recalled Philippians 4:8–9, "Whatever is true... honorable... right... pure... lovely... whatever is of good repute, if there is any excellence and if anything worthy of praise, dwell on these things... practice these things, and the God of peace will be with you" (NASB).

She decided to call them and bring the overpayment to their attention. They admitted it was a mistake, were grateful for her honesty, and asked her to kindly mail the check back in exchange for the correct one, which she did. A week later, she received a phone call from a large church, inviting her to speak for their women's group. They offered a generous honorarium that exceeded the check she had mailed back to the conference. She gladly accepted.

25

The whole month of May is like a dogfight between good and evil in my head — the anniversary of the day Jim and I met, our wedding anniversary, and Jim's birthday. Sometimes I don't even want to get up in the morning — I just want to cry all day long, because I really miss Jim. But I climb out of bed, put on the shoes of peace, open my Bible to the gospel of Matthew, and the Lord speaks to me through His Word. He says, "Lo, *I am* with you always, even to the end of the age" (Matthew 28:20, NASB) [emphasis mine]. What a comfort to know that *He is*.

Many days at the pharmacy are absolute chaos. I remember one particular day when phones were ringing, computers were crashing, customers were complaining, cashiers called out sick, and I had a splitting headache. The enemy hurled all kinds of challenges at me, hoping I'd succumb to my short temper and make a bad situation even worse. Instead, I chose to incorporate Paul's military strategy. I made a deliberate effort to remain calm, smile a lot, and do the best I could without a computer. I kept reciting Psalm 25:21 in my mind: "May integrity and uprightness protect me, because my hope is in You" (NIV). Before I knew it, the day was over and I was home enjoying a hot cup of tea.

Another day at the pharmacy, a customer at the counter asked to see the pharmacist, so I went out to help him. He pulled seven prescription bottles out of his coat pocket and told me he was having trouble figuring out which pills to take at what time. I took a sheet of paper and made a detailed chart for him — listing his morning meds, afternoon meds, and night meds. He was thrilled. He thanked me and said, "How much do I owe you?"

I grinned and said, "Don't be silly. That's what I'm here for." He couldn't believe that a pharmacist's time, knowledge, and advice were free.

"*Nothing* in this world is free!" he insisted.

That gave me a very brief chance to put on the helmet of salvation and tell him, "Not true. The gift of eternal life is free." Turns out that his wife was trying to convince him to come to church with her, and he's thinking about it.

All Scripture is inspired by God; its purpose is to give us protection, correction, and direction (2 Timothy 3:16) and I enjoy memorizing it. I never would have believed that I'd develop such a passion for it, but I can truly say that ever since I've immersed myself in the Bible, my life has been so much simpler and more tolerable. As soon as I'm confronted with a challenge, I pull one of my favorite Bible passages out of my mental repertoire and recite it in my mind until it gives me a sense of peace... and it works, *every time.*

By the way... ever since I lost Jim, I've started a new tradition. Each year on May 27th, I return to the restaurant where we met and I place a single red rose in the parking space where Jim and I smiled at each other and shook hands for the first time. However, I am no longer overcome by the evil of anguish or the temptation of despair... instead I praise God for arranging that meeting between us, and I thank Him for making me teachable.

·tf·

Every good and perfect gift is from above, coming down from the Father of the heavenly lights, who does not change like shifting shadows.

~James 1:17 (NIV)

Vision
Test

7

I realize now that I loved Jim far more than I loved God. It took me awhile to recognize this, but accepting it and admitting it was another huge step in my journey.

But he was your husband, you might say. *You're supposed to love, honor, and cherish him.* Indeed that is true, and indeed I did. But I also put Jim in the center of my life and my field of vision — and that was wrong. I broke the first commandment: "You shall have no other gods before me" (Exodus 20:3, KJV). There are many obvious gods and false idols in this world — the god of money, the god of luxury, the god of status, the god of alcohol or drugs — and many people worship them instead of the One true God. Jim was my god; he was my idol. He was a gift to me, but I loved the gift more than the Giver of that gift. I even blatantly stated that every morning for five years in my prayer to God when Jim left for work: "Please, Lord, get Jim to work safely and bring him home safely, too... *because he's everything in the world to me* and I love him so much." In the corporation of my life, Jim held a much higher position than God did.

No, God does not demand that a certain percentage of our thoughts be consumed with Him... we don't punch a time clock. Yes, He surely must have been proud of the love that Jim and I had for each other — after all, it was God Himself who gave it to us. And God is certainly not saying that we should not love everyone in our life; in fact, He commands us to love them. I'm not saying that I should have loved Jim any less than I did. But the fact of the matter is that I cared far more about my relationship with my husband than my relationship with my Creator.

Everything good that we have, everything good that we see, exists because of God (check it out in James 1:17). Everything from the bright sun in the sky to that cool new lamp from Pier 1. Everything from the majesty of the ocean to that bottle of Poland Spring water. Everything from the endless green fields of corn to that bag of Fritos corn chips. And then, of course, there's Jesus.

How do we even begin to thank Jesus for the gift of His life and His sacrifice for our salvation? We can live our lives loving, trusting, and obeying Him... but it still doesn't even come close to reciprocating what He did — and still does — for us. He gives us His endless love, His infinite grace, His abounding mercy, His constant faithfulness, His tireless patience, His radical forgiveness. And that's just the beginning. He asks so little of us, and we give Him so little... yet He gives so much in return. Lucky for us He's not keeping score.

God constantly provides us with presents as if every day is our birthday. Sometimes He delivers them as a direct shipment from the throne, like those gasp-out-loud pink and purple sunsets. Other times, He uses a courier service — like the neighbor who brought you dinner when you broke your arm and couldn't cook. Our families, our friends, our health, our homes, our freedom, our cars, our jobs — they're all blessings and gifts from above given from our Father who loves to give.

But where do those gifts appear in our field of vision? What do we spend more time focusing on? When we peek through an optical lens at our lives, what do we see? (Caution: Objects in mirror are closer than they appear!) When we look at the eye chart of our priorities, what figure stands out like the big, bold *E* on the top line?

When I asked myself those questions some time after 9/11 and answered them honestly, the truth alarmed me. That's when I realized that Jim was clearly in the foreground, while God was barely visible in the periphery. There was a giant *J* on the top line of my eye chart... but it didn't stand for Jesus.

Jim was a precious gift to me, but he was on loan. For a long time, I didn't understand that. Removing Jim from my vision forced me to focus on God... whether it was through the eyes of anger and bitterness (as it was in the beginning) or the eyes of praise and adoration (as it is now). Either way, I noticed Him.

Unfortunately it took a tragedy for that to happen. But because of that tragedy, I can see more clearly. Is my vision 20/20 now? No, and it won't be — until the day I stand before the Divine Ophthalmologist and He perfects it. But it's amazing what a pair of corrective lenses will do for our spiritual eyesight...

·tf·

The sovereign LORD *has given me an instructed tongue, to know the word that sustains the weary...*

~Isaiah 50:4 (NIV)

Oral
Exams

8

When churches began asking me to verbally share my testimony after *A Tempered Faith* was released, my first reaction was to veto the idea. Recall that I had no experience speaking in front of any audience about any subject, ever.

> *There is no way that I can talk about this in front of a crowd! I am not strong enough to maintain my emotional composure. I mean, it's not like I'm getting up there to talk about bicycle repair or pharmaceuticals.*

My publisher's reply? "Jen, you said the same thing about writing the book."

Yeah, well, that was different. I'm a much better writer than I am a speaker. Anyone can see that just by having a conversation with me. And besides, I have a really close relationship with the delete and the backspace keys. I'm fond of them, and they're good to me. Unfortunately, I can't take them with me when I step up to the podium.

> *Lord, is it really necessary for me to get up there*

33

in front of all those people and talk about this?
You know I'm not an eloquent speaker — I'm
sure I'll freeze up and get tongue-tied.

Hmmmm, that sounds familiar. Didn't Moses say something
like that when God asked him to address His people?

Yes, Lord, by Your grace, I wrote A Tempered
Faith. It was healing for me, and hopefully it is
healing for others. I will be forever grateful to You
for giving me that opportunity to share my story.
But maybe we should just do a few more book
signings and be done with it. You are taking me
way outside the safety of my comfort zone with
this public speaking thing.

I wondered what God had to say to Moses about his reluctance
for public speaking. I found it in Exodus 4:12: "Now go; I will
help you speak and will teach you what to say" (NIV). In the re-
cesses of my heart, I felt the gentle nudging of the Holy Spirit.
He was saying, "Trust Me. Have I ever failed you? Please trust
Me. You won't be alone in front of any audience, ever. Trust Me.
We have more work to do — we're not finished. Just trust Me."

And so I did. And He once again proved Himself to be the
Almighty One.

The very first time I spoke in front of an audience was in a
small church in Pennsylvania late in the summer of 2003 during
their 9:00 A.M. Sunday service. I had practiced this presentation
for weeks beforehand at home. I received advice, guidance, and
coaching from my brother-in-law Tom, but never once had I
made it through without freezing or fumbling. I prayed about it,

34

but the instruction of 1 Peter 5:7, "casting my anxiety upon Him," was much easier said than done.

The congregation was a warm, loving, and receptive crowd, but I was still queasy and trembling as I stepped up to the pulpit with my notes. What happened next was something I had heard other speakers describe, but I truly never believed was possible — until it happened to me. The words were flowing out of my mouth (all the correct words, by the way), but my mind was not concentrating on them. It felt like my brain was on pause, and someone else was at the control panel... and I know now in my heart that it was the Holy Spirit. After an emotional and virtually flawless twenty-minute testimony, I finished... and I felt as if a tremendous weight had been lifted. It wasn't me. It was God, and He had successfully pulled it off with flying colors.

And just as I was exhaling the biggest sigh of relief, the pastor eagerly asked if I would speak for the 11:00 A.M. service also. *You mean I have to do this all over again?! What if God thinks I can manage it all by myself now?*

That day, God once again made it indisputably clear to me that He *is* in control. He took me outside of my comfort zone and showed me that it wasn't as painful as I had anticipated. He expanded my limits and unveiled another gift that I didn't even know existed. He proved to me that I need to trust Him to finish the job that He started in me.

I continue to experience His awesome power every time I give my testimony. My program has changed quite a bit since that first church in Pennsylvania; the message has greatly expanded and is now accompanied by a full slideshow and videos. And it's a family road show: Maria is my multimedia engineer, my personal assistant, and my traveling companion. Tom has been my consultant, my sound man, and my booking agent. Mom is my official bookseller, Dad is the roadie for my equip-

35

ment, and they both serve as my caterers — complete with delivery service. My family's help and their support of my speaking ministry are priceless, and I could not do it without them. I prepare to speak *as if* it will depend on us — knowing with full confidence that it will ultimately depend on God.

God gently and patiently teaches me with each presentation by giving me an assortment of challenges to see how I'll handle them. In doing so, He refines my skills. The presentations aren't always smooth; they aren't always easy; they aren't always perfect. In fact, some have been downright frustrating. But the feedback from the audience is always positive, because the outcome is *always* His.

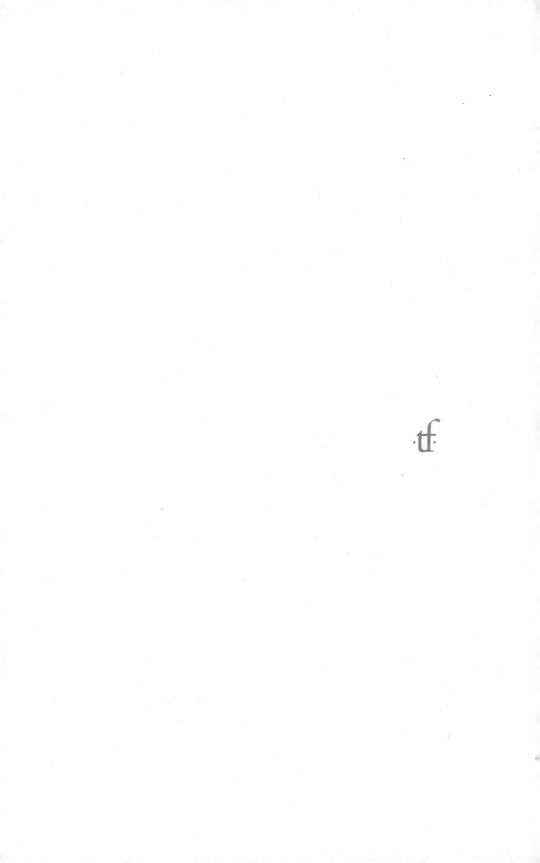

For our light and momentary troubles are achieving for us an eternal glory that far outweighs them all.

~2 Corinthians 4:17 (NIV)

Class
Clown

9

Speaking at major bookstore chains can often be a challenge for me. Apparently, God doesn't see it that way. To Him, it's an opportunity to take me out of my comfort zone yet again and force me to confront my fears, because He knows I have to get over it. One of those fears is speaking to an audience in an uncontrolled retail environment and not being able to concentrate. There is always the possibility of screaming children, cell phones ringing, and overhead intercom announcements. On one particular occasion, I was handed all of them in their full glory...

In this busy store, the children's book section was located directly behind where I was speaking — only a small bookcase divided the two areas. During the first twenty minutes of my presentation, there were several children in full playground mode — complete with barking, squealing, and chanting. They were also armed with some kind of digital instruments that continually beeped and honked and whistled.

Then, their father's cell phone rang to the tune of "Yankee Doodle." And it rang. And rang. And rang. I was just about ready to scream, "Can you *please* answer your phone?" when he did. And I'm so sorry he did. Because he then proceeded to talk the way that a person talks when they have headphones on, totally unaware of the volume of their voice. The audience and I heard his entire conversation, since he vocally projected over his children and through an apparently bad cell phone connection. He made plans for the holiday weekend, complained about his neighbor's lumber encroaching upon *his* driveway, and expressed a strong desire to have salami and provolone for lunch.

Just as the event coordinator walked over to ask him to lower his voice, they left. Dad was still yelling into his cell phone as he walked down the aisle heading for the door with his kinder-garten clan following behind.

Yes, kids will be kids. Yes, he had just as much right to be in that store as we did. And yes, he may have been oblivious to my program. But it just kills me. *I'm talkin' here.*

Then there was the overhead intercom. Unavoidable, I under-stand. It's a necessary form of communication so that a retail business runs smoothly. But instead of the cashier calmly an-nouncing, "Manager, line three, please," we heard, "I NEED A MANAGER, PHONE CALL, PICK UP LINE THREE, CUSTOMER WAITING FOR A MANAGER!!" And this happened not once, not twice, not three times, but four times while I was speaking (different demands with each announce-ment). Each time, I had to stop mid-sentence and wait for the overhead voice to cease fire before I could continue.

Miraculously, I made it through the program without fum-bling, losing my place, or having a total brain freeze. If God wasn't running that show, then I'm packin' it in… because there is *no* other explanation that I can accept *and* be comfortable with.

Sometimes the challenges come in the form of mechanical failures — like the time that I was the keynote speaker at a din-ner for an honorary women educator's group. The first problem I encountered was with my laptop and projector, which I use for my slideshow presentation and videos. Maria runs the multime-

40

dia while I speak, and we had used this equipment successfully many times before. But on this particular night, for some strange reason we have yet to determine, the images on the projection screen had a hideous green tint. No matter what we tried, we could not get rid of it, and the entire hour-long visual presentation looked like... well... algae.

I gritted my teeth and began the program anyway, apologizing for the nauseating color on the screen. Then, about five minutes into the presentation, my lapel microphone batteries went dead. This was *my* microphone and *my* negligence, so I couldn't even blame it on anyone else. I really wanted to just wave buh-bye, exit the premises immediately, and move to Albuquerque. But since there was no other sound system in place and since the show must go on, I had to pull out the old Italian grandmother voice. I had to speak louder than I do when I'm talking to Mr. Smith (who is hard of hearing) at the pharmacy about how to take his medicine. Since I always have a microphone, I'm not accustomed to projecting my voice to a crowd... and there are times when my voice needs to be soft. For instance, one cannot bellow at the top of one's lungs: "But Jim never came home that day..."

About five minutes after I lost the microphone, the air conditioning went on full blast and stayed on. Now I was competing with a thirty-year-old compressor that sounded like a lawnmower. I also had a cougher in the audience. She was coughing up a lung for what seemed like an eternity... but did she excuse herself? Nooooo. So, there was a hacking woman, a 200-decibel air conditioner, a funky green screen, and I had no sound system.

But the good news is, I got through it by the grace of God. What did He teach me from it? Change microphone batteries before *every* presentation. Hire an MIT computer engineer graduate to attend every program at whatever price he asks. And

41

carry cough drops and practice aiming and tossing them at the offender's mouth.

All kidding aside, the most important thing I have learned — from the minor annoyances at my presentations to the major crises of my life — is that they shape my character and make me stronger. They equip me to face more challenges in the future. God allows distress in our lives because it teaches us to become dependent on Him, which in turn cements our spiritual foundation. James 1:2–3 says: "Consider it all joy, my brethren, when you encounter various trials, knowing that the testing of your faith produces endurance" (NASB). The trials never seem like gifts at the time... but in hindsight, we can often see how the outcome teaches us, equips us, benefits us, and glorifies God.

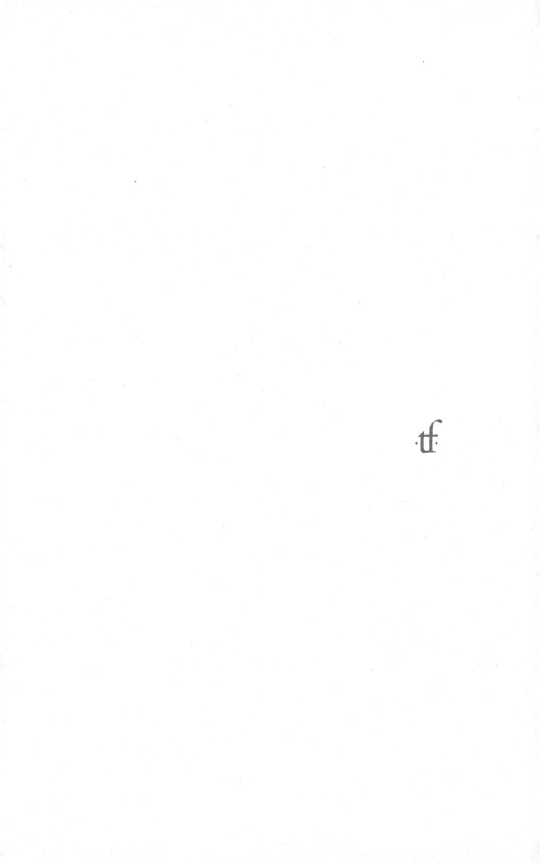

...be prepared in season and out of season; correct, rebuke and encourage — with great patience and careful instruction.

~2 Timothy 4:2 (NIV)

Computer
Science

10

Digitally, I had it made — I was married to a computer genius. I was spoiled, and I had no interest in learning any more than the basics on the computer since Jim could make things happen with the snap of a finger. Our small home office with Jim's network of computers looked like IBM headquarters. Even with air-conditioning, the office was always eighty degrees or higher and emitted an eerie glow — like a nuclear power plant. There were five different computer systems and a tangled mass of cables and connections all snarled together in one corner of the room. Whenever I caught a glimpse of that electrical anarchy, I would gasp in horror.

After September 11th, I was lost in cyberspace. I knew how to do simple things like send and receive email, but that was the extent of my computer ability. With the amount of email I was receiving immediately after the terrorist attacks, I soon found myself spending a good deal of time on the computer.

Eventually, Jim's friend Marc came to the rescue and dismantled four out of the five systems, which simplified my life. My nephew Kevin (Maria and Tom's older son) followed in Jim's footsteps and now develops software for the financial industry in New York (Jim would be so proud of him), so we thankfully once again have a computer engineer in the family. Kevin and

Marc have both bailed me out of many hair-pulling electronic predicaments.

The computer soon evolved into my link with the rest of the world. It allowed me to communicate with other 9/11 family members, with distant family and friends, even with complete strangers around the country and the world. Everyone offered their support and condolences, and they all played an integral role in my healing process.

Yet I've learned that total reliance on electronics can be dangerous. There was a time — not so long ago — when computers did not exist and everyone made it through each day just fine. Now, if I am without a functioning system for even an hour, it's a major crisis. I discovered that unhealthy dependence a few months ago when my computer crashed at a most inopportune time — during the writing of this book.

Kevin and Marc were not around to rescue me, so I called technical support. They routed my call to a barely-English-speaking representative with a conveniently English-sounding name: Cindy. After three hours of troubleshooting the problem, Cindy instructed me to disassemble the computer's tower (I thought she was kidding — she wasn't) in order to "re-seat the memory boards." This was not going to be an easy task given the facts that:

1. I am very computer illiterate
2. We had a serious language barrier

Nevertheless, I did successfully open the tower and look inside at the guts of my computer, feeling as incompetent as a manicurist trying to perform an appendectomy. I was having difficulty locating those memory boards (big surprise!), because I had no clue what they looked like. Cindy told me to look for "four green tabs, because they are attached to the memory boards." I searched. There were no green tabs anywhere. She kept repeating herself — "locate the four green tabs" — as if her repetition would make me find it more quickly. I kept repeating myself — "there *are no* green tabs" — and wishing so much that Jim was here to fix this himself. My futile search and our redundant dialogue continued for another thirty minutes. Finally I said, "Wait a minute. Are you saying *green* tabs, as in G-R-E-E-N?"

Cindy answered with her thick accent rather matter-of-factly. "No, Ma'am. They are cream, as in C-R-E-A-M."

My blood boiled. "*Cream?* As in... *white?!*"

"Yes, Ma'am," she replied, even more matter-of-factly.

I lost it.

"*SO, WHY DIDN'T YOU JUST SAY WHITE?! Okay, now I see them!*" The only thing that stopped me from swearing was my fleeting thought that perhaps Jesus and Jim were both sitting on the floor with me — looking at computer parts sprawled all over the place — and thoroughly enjoying this episode of *I Love Lucy* starring Jennifer Sands.

My computer was eventually fixed and no data was lost, and I thank and praise God for the lessons He taught me.

He taught me patience. Cindy was doing her job and was trying her best to help me. Her difficulty in communicating was no reason to blow my testimony.

He taught me perseverance. I knew in my heart that eventually the computer would be fixed and that I had to trust God to work it all out somehow. After all, He certainly knows how important a computer is to my ministry. He wasn't going to leave me without one forever.

He taught me dependence... on Christ, not on computers. Sure, it's nice to have them and they really make our lives easier (when they work), but computers aren't life-support equipment

47

(though many people would disagree with me). The Bible was hand-written by scribes on scrolls of parchment. If absolutely necessary, this book *could have been* written with a ballpoint pen on loose-leaf notebook paper. But God was gracious, and He once again provided me with functioning hardware and software to complete the manuscript.

Since 9/11, there has been no rest for my computer. With the release of *A Tempered Faith* came the emergence of my website, www.jennifersands.com. I am sure that Jim is up there doubled over in laughter because his computer-illiterate wife has her own website. And he's probably telling everyone the story about the time that *I* insisted to *him* — you know, the computer genius — that *Microsoft* was a fabric related to silk.

I receive large volumes of email every day through the website, and I reply to countless people who reach out to me in their darkest hours. It didn't take me long to realize that God had placed me in a strategic position. He had planted so many strangers in my life to pull me away from the edge of the Black Hole. And now He was planting me into other people's lives to help pull them away from theirs. Before I knew it, jennifersands.com became a private and anonymous support system for many distressed individuals. In 2 Corinthians 1:3–4, Paul refers to "...the God of all comfort, who comforts us in all our troubles, so that we can comfort those in any trouble with the comfort we ourselves have received from God" (NIV). Suffering isn't only used for our own spiritual growth; it is also used to benefit others.

The website became proof of 2 Corinthians 1:3 with a Pentium 4 processor — online, on duty, and ongoing...

·ʈf·

If any of you lacks wisdom, he should ask God, who gives generously to all without finding fault, and it will be given to him.

~James 1:5 (NIV)

SATs

11

I was always a good student in school — the kind that parents brag about and other kids beat you up for. National Honor Society throughout high school, *Magna Cum Laude* throughout college. But my scores were terrible on my SATs: my Spiritual Aptitude Tests. I assumed I had mastered the curriculum since I had perfect attendance in church every Sunday. I donated money and old clothes to good causes and returned lost wallets to their rightful owner, hoping to score a few points with the Teacher.

But the truth is that my knowledge of the Bible was restricted to what I had learned from Andrew Lloyd Weber. Thanks to *Joseph and the Amazing Technicolor Dreamcoat*, I could proudly recite the names of all twelve of Jacob's sons. And sure, I prayed to God... when I needed something. Otherwise, He was incidental, and I made Him wait on the sidelines.

I think back to those early days after 9/11, and I cringe when I think about my anger at God and how I blamed Him. Yes, God understood and expected me to have that reaction when my world was falling apart, but does that mean I was entitled to feel that way? Did I earn my right to be angry with Him? Nope. *I* was the one who hadn't played by the rules — God always had.

It was *my* responsibility to comprehend the Word of God and how He works... but I never studied for that exam.

> *Do I read the Bible? I don't need a Bible; I go to church. Am I saved? I don't need to be saved; I'm not a sinner. Never killed anyone, never committed adultery, always honored my mother and father. Deceit? God doesn't mind when we lie once in a while — it's always for a good reason, anyway. Idolatry? Of course I know what that means... it's worshiping other gods, like in Greek mythology. I don't worship Neptune or Aphrodite. I worship God — for one whole hour every Sunday morning.*

There was so much I did not understand — so much that I took for granted or never even bothered to inquire about; so much that I callously disregarded, assuming it was irrelevant to my life; so much that I misunderstood in my shortsightedness and ignorance. For instance, I had heard that God was a "jealous" God, and that was a scary and unsettling thought for someone who did not understand the context and biblical translation of the word *jealous*. I now understand that it refers to idolatry and means that God does not want us to place more significance on anyone or anything else than on Him. He created the universe. He has rightfully earned His place in the front of the line.

Then I discovered that the biblical use of the word *hate* (as in "hate the world") does not mean to have strong negative feelings about the world; it simply means "do not become attached to the world" (since we'll be leaving it one day). And then there's the word *fear* (as in "fear the Lord"), which does not mean to be afraid of the Lord; it means to highly respect Him... Wow... Imagine

52

what we can learn about God if we just spend some quality time with Him, if we get to know Him through His Word, if we desire to become teachable.

There were many Scripture passages that were confusing and disturbing for me, since I had no biblical foundation whatsoever. Some verses were downright terrifying, like, "If your foot causes you to stumble, cut it off" (Mark 9:45, NASB), or, "For whoever wishes to save his life will lose it" (Matthew 16:25, NASB). The first time I read Romans 5:3, I was floored. "We also rejoice in our sufferings" (NIV). Huh? What is *that* all about? I'm hurting and I'm not happy about it!

This reminds me of when I was eight years old and my best friend developed a case of ringworm. Ringworm? Ugh! I wouldn't go near her for months. It wasn't until I went to pharmacy school fifteen years later that I learned that ringworm isn't a worm at all. It's a common fungal infection that's easily treatable and not transmittable by human contact. Time, experience, and knowledge all bring forth an understanding of things that we were once too immature to comprehend. And of course, the Lord teaches us when we seek Him with all our heart — when we desire to become teachable.

My SAT scores have improved dramatically since that first exposure to Jeremiah 29:11 on the Salvation Army card... but I'm certainly no Bible scholar. And I definitely don't have all the answers — I still have a lot more to learn. This earth is a perpetual classroom, and we are all perpetually students. As for me, I started out majoring in anger and depression. I eventually switched majors along the way, and now I'm working on my Master's degree in faith and trust in God. I know that by following, trusting, and obeying the Teacher, I will one day put on my cap and white robe; and He will hand me my diploma as He says, "Well done, My good and faithful servant." I can't wait for graduation day...

53

And whatever you do, do it heartily, as to the Lord and not to men, knowing that from the Lord you will receive the reward of the inheritance...
~Colossians 3:23–24 (NKJV)

Making the Grade

12

From the age of ten through the age of eighteen, I took piano lessons every single week. My fascination with the piano began early in life as I listened to my older brother Anthony play. As an exceptional and accomplished pianist, he could play any song on earth — without sheet music — if you simply hummed the tune for him. Anthony has *the gift*.

Here's an illustration of Anthony's brilliance. In the early 1970s, he played a distinguished solo for a prestigious concert at a large outdoor auditorium in front of a very big audience. Halfway through his performance, a strong wind came along and blew his sheet music right off the piano and onto the stage. The entire audience — including my family and me — gasped out loud in horror and held their breath. But Anthony calmly continued to play, never missing a note, as if nothing had happened. He played from his memory and from his heart. Someone backstage realized the potential calamity and ran out, retrieved the music, and placed it back on the piano's music stand. Anthony told us later that although this person's efforts were well intended, they were in vain. The man had placed the music in front of my brother *upside down*. Even so, Anthony finished his performance flawlessly and received a standing ovation.

He never pursued music as a career. Instead, Anthony became a successful professional thoroughbred jockey for many years. Then, being an overachiever, he went to medical school and eventually became Dr. Anthony Trebino, anesthesiologist. He practiced medicine for many years before his life tragically changed.

In July of 2000, Anthony was diagnosed with a terminal brain tumor. After three major surgeries, months of chemotherapy and radiation, numerous complications, and a very poor prognosis, he blew away the odds. He has not only survived, but he has triumphed over the greatest personal misfortune of his life. He is a living, breathing, walking miracle — an answer to so many prayers and another amazing example of how God can take a tragedy and turn it into a victory. Anthony's faith in God never faltered throughout his entire ordeal... instead, it became deeper and stronger... and he became teachable.

Today, Anthony and his beautiful wife Carla — who is a precious blessing to all of us and another answer to our prayers — live each day with joy and good health, always aware of God's grace and mercy. And miraculously, even after the harsh trauma to the frontal and left temporal lobes of his brain, Anthony's gift for playing the piano was preserved. He can still produce the sweetest music from those keys with or without the sheet music in front of him.

So it was the sound of my brother's music — and the impression left on me after that infamously windy concert — that prompted me to start taking piano lessons in 1974. I soon discovered that unlike my brother, I did *not* have *the gift*. Unlike Anthony, the notes did not come naturally and instinctively. I played very well, but I had to work hard at it. And my ultimate downfall? The demand I placed upon myself for complete perfection and the endless time and effort I put forth to accomplish that perfection. In my idealistic mind, a piece was not deemed worthy

unless it was played flawlessly. I would play a sixteen-page over-
ture, and if I hit a wrong chord anywhere along the way, my
compulsive nature would not allow me to just pick up after the
clinker and keep going... No way. I had to stop and play the entire song all over again from the very beginning, and I would play
it as many times as it took until I got every single note absolutely
perfect. Only then would I be happy.

Here's an illustration of *my* brilliance. After eight years of rig-
orous lessons and intense practice and many concerts of my
own, I had finally achieved an advanced skill level that may have
gotten me accepted into Juilliard if I was interested... which I
wasn't. In 1982 as the final soloist at a recital, I played *Rhapsody
in Blue* — all thirty-one grueling pages and thirty exhausting
minutes of it — as flawlessly as George Gershwin himself could
have ever hoped for. After pounding out those final, closing,
thunderous B-flats that end the performance, I was emotionally
and physically drained. All the time and effort I had put forth in
the past eight years had reached its peak, and I was done. It was
over. Not simply the recital itself but the entire musical realm of
my life. It just became too hard, too demanding, too stressful...
and I just didn't want it anymore. I got up, took my bow, ac-
knowledged the gracious audience, then walked off the stage.
Outwardly, I was smiling but deep inside I had emphatically
made up my mind. *That's it. No more. I'm never doing this
again. That's the last time I am putting my fingers on a piano.*
And I meant it.

My parents were crushed. My piano teacher was horrified.
Everyone told me I'd regret that decision one day, and they were
right. Ten years went by, and I had kept my promise of never
once touching a piano. Eventually, my fingers became restless,
and in the depths of my heart, I felt a tugging to experience
those keys again. But unlike riding a bike, you cannot just sit

down at a piano after a ten-year hiatus and pick up where you left off. I tried to play again, but I instantly discovered what I had feared — I had lost the skill that I once worked so hard for. Getting it back would require starting over again with intense practice and study. I was discouraged, frustrated, and angry with myself for that earlier defiance and for throwing in the towel when I should have held onto it. Today, I will occasionally fool around and plink out some notes — as long as no one is around to hear it, for the humiliation is unbearable.

In my house sits a magnificent, black Otto Altenburg full grand piano... it is very lonely and rarely gets played unless Anthony comes over to give it the love and attention it so rightfully deserves.

People would visit our home and say, "Wow, beautiful piano! Who plays?" And Jim would answer, "Jennifer *allegedly* plays, but I won't believe it until I hear it." Poor Jim never heard any attempt on my part to prove otherwise... although I think that was in the best interest of his ears. However, some time after 9/11, I sat down alone at the piano one day and played Elton John's "Your Song." In my mind I sang the song, but I slightly changed the words: "I hope you don't mind, I hope you don't mind, that I put down in words, how wonderful life was, while you were in the world."

I played it — complete with dreadful clinkers and awful blunders, horrendously fumbling and crying through the whole thing. When it was over, I said, "There Hon, you finally heard me play. Now do you believe me?" And I envisioned Jim's smart aleck grin and his comeback of something like, "Yeah, I believe you. And I'm thinkin' maybe you should reimburse your parents for all the money they invested in those lessons."

As I look back now, I realize that God used those piano recitals to prepare me for appearing in front of audiences twenty-five years later. He enabled me to gain confidence back then; and even when I ran away from it, He eventually called me back to the task later on… in a different way, for a different purpose. For *His* purpose.

In Paul's letter to the Colossians, he wrote, "And whatever you do, do it heartily, as to the Lord and not to men" (Colossians 3:23, NKJV). Notice how Paul says that whatever we do in life, we should do it *heartily* — not *perfectly*. We must strive to do our best; we must not become lazy or apathetic; we must put our heart into everything we do — knowing that we will not always be perfect and that our imperfection may result in disappointment, rejection, or sin. But whatever we do, we must do it *heartily*.

For most of my life, I tried heartily to be perfect, and I inflicted that quest upon others — *I've decided we're having Thanksgiving at my house. Be here at two o'clock sharp, bring a dessert, and stay out of the kitchen.*

I was a bona fide control freak, and I excelled in the sport. My personality was such that I had to maintain control over every situation and circumstance in my life, lest I self-destruct. I made plans, I lived by them, and I was frustrated if they were changed or interrupted. *What do you mean, the carpet cleaner can't come till next week? That's not acceptable. He'll come tomorrow, or I'll find someone else.* For thirty-seven years, I assumed — with so much certainty — that I was running the show.

Then came 9/11, and I discovered that I didn't have as much control over my life as I thought I had.

I knew I had to re-train my mind and my actions, so I checked myself into perfectionist and control-freak detox. I had to accept that my family, friends, and God will still love me even when I'm not perfect and that I cannot always have my way. I had to learn total submission to God; I had to learn His Word; I had to conform to His Will; I had to become teachable.

At this point in my life, I'm trying to perfect the art of *not* being perfect, especially when it's *not* important to *be* perfect. (Did you get that?)

Fortunately God doesn't deal with us the way we deal with ourselves. And fortunately, He will disregard all our clinkers and fumbles, and we will have the chance to present ourselves before the Throne with a perfect score. Philippians 1:6 says, "For I am confident of this very thing, that He who began a good work in you will perfect it until the day of Christ Jesus" (NASB).

I'm sure glad that God is the Perfectionist, not me.

And do not be conformed to this world, but be transformed by the renewing of your mind; so that you may prove what the will of God is, that which is good and acceptable and perfect.

~Romans 12:2 (NASB)

Home Ec.

13

Jim often joked that I was happiest when I was eating. Actually, I think he was right. God knows this too, and so He likes to use food to teach me more about Him. He sure knows how to speak my language.

Eleanor Roosevelt said, "A woman is like a tea bag. You never know how strong she is until she gets into hot water." Here, here, Eleanor. And that little bit o' wisdom goes for you gentlemen too.

Sometimes we are submerged into the scalding water of grief, pain, heartache, disappointment, and failure. But we can surface from the depths radically improved if we will simply trust and allow God to bring about His improvements. And as a result of our trials, we might even be able to make a small difference in the world around us. What we're made of can determine what we become when the heat is turned up.

Put a tea bag into a mug full of boiling water.

Put a cup of rice in a pot of boiling water.

Observe.

The rice started out hard and unfit to eat, but after it was subjected to the boiling water, it became softened and edible.

After the tea bag steeped for a while, it changed the hot water — it altered the surrounding conditions.

Both faced the same extreme circumstances — boiling water — yet they reacted differently.

Even if we can't change our circumstances, we can change the way we respond to them. Like the rice, the challenges in our life can be an opportunity to improve ourselves. Like a tea bag, sometimes we can use the challenges to improve the world around us.

Or… maybe we can even do both. Bring out the instant oatmeal.

It starts out in dry powder form and is fairly useful in cookie recipes. But when it comes in contact with hot water, the oatmeal transforms *and* so does the water. Together, the dry oatmeal and the boiling water (with a sprinkle of sugar and cinnamon) evolve into someone's delicious and nourishing breakfast.

I want to be that oatmeal. I want the trials in my life to make me more useful to God and more palatable and edifying to others. And I want the result of my trials to somehow make a positive difference in the world. I like the way the apostle Peter said it: "In this you greatly rejoice, even though now for a little while, if necessary, you have been distressed by various trials, so that the proof of your faith… even though tested by fire, may be found to result in praise and glory and honor at the revelation of Jesus Christ" (1 Peter 1:6–7, NASB).

I don't think Peter was thinking about food when he wrote that, but he might have agreed with my philosophy — tea bags, rice, oatmeal, hot water, our hearts, our heartaches, our minds, our lives — God can transform it all… *if* we let Him.

And I am absolutely sure that Jim is rolling his eyes at me right now with all this talk about food.

I remember a visitor I had a few weeks after September 11th. Mary (not her real name) was young, and she had already been a widow for several years. Her husband was a police officer who had been shot and killed in the line of duty. She ultimately became involved with gun control laws, and she started a bereavement group in her church. Someone in Jim's family knew her and asked her to come to my house to talk to me. I can still clearly recall her standing in front of me, holding both of my hands as I sobbed uncontrollably. And with a smile of confidence, she said, "Jennifer, you *are* going to be okay. Just keep your faith and focus on God, and I promise you, it *will* be okay!"

I also remember thinking to myself, *Yeah right, lady. You obviously have no idea how happy I was and how unhappy I am now. Yes, I know you lost your husband too, but apparently you guys didn't have the relationship that Jim and I did, or maybe you're just a lot stronger than I am. So don't make me any promises and don't talk to me about God. Just go away.*

That was the last time I saw Mary. I hear her name every once in a while because she's still involved with bereavement support groups and gun control laws. Mary is a perfect example of instant oatmeal. She was immersed in the scorching water of tragedy; and she not only emerged a stronger person, but God uses her to bring comfort to others and to make the world a safer place. I did not believe her words back then... but now I know she was speaking the truth... and she was teaching me.

tf

"...for they all shall know Me, from the least of them to the greatest of them," says the LORD. *"For I will forgive their iniquity, and their sin I will remember no more."*

~Jeremiah 31:34 (NKJV)

Erasers

14

For a long time, I despised Tuesdays and the eleventh of every month. And I would find myself recalling exactly what Jim and I were doing at a certain time or on a certain day when he was alive. *Exactly five years ago today, we were in Aruba. We were in our hotel room, having just finished a late dinner at our favorite restaurant. The power went out just before midnight, and the entire island was pitch black.*

In the early days after 9/11, thinking about that nostalgic memory would have caused me to burst into tears. Now, through the grace of God, I think about it and burst into laughter, especially when I remember how Jim walked smack into the sliding glass door on his way out to the balcony (he forgot the door was closed and couldn't see anything in the dark). There eventually came a time when the memories didn't hurt anymore... and now, I thirst for them.

I remember the first time I went food shopping after Jim died. It was traumatic. In *A Tempered Faith*, I referred to these events as Reality Bricks — sudden, painful reminders that Jim was no longer here. Every aisle was an emotional land mine of Jim's favorite snacks. I took a deep breath and did what I went in there to do. I like the way my sister-in-law Carla illustrates it:

"You took that Reality Brick, grabbed it by the collar, and shook it. And it shook you up a bit too, but the fact is that you defeated the Reality Brick... it did not defeat you." It's like that with everything we must face. What's the alternative? To *never* go food shopping again? To *never* go to the movies again? To *never* go to the beach, or to ball games, or *anywhere* that will trigger painful reminders that our loved ones can no longer share these places with us? Those are not reasonable options; in fact, they're not options at all. The more often I went to the store (or anywhere), the easier it became. It's a process of desensitization, and God helped me to overcome the Reality Bricks.

God gives us an amazing and fascinating gift of memory. Certain memories are tattooed in our minds, and we cannot erase them. We can catch a glimpse of something — or a familiar smell — and we will be spontaneously transported back in time to when that memory took place. Memories can be rich blessings... like our favorite childhood vacation spot and the smell of cotton candy on the boardwalk.

But even the painful memories that torment our minds — like an image of a commercial airliner crashing into a skyscraper, which in turn triggers terrifying thoughts about where our loved ones might be spending eternity — can be blessings in disguise. How? By confronting those thoughts and images and allowing God to heal you through it and to help you grow from it.

I had to confront my concerns about whether or not Jim was in heaven... they were thoughts that consumed my mind and tortured me for so long. But God has given me a peace about it, and I no longer worry about Jim's eternal status. First of all, there is absolutely nothing I can do to change it. And I've finally learned that worrying about something I have no control over is not only fruitless but destructive.

We are all sinners. I am; Jim was. Among other things, he un-

68

doubtedly practiced the same form of idolatry as I did. Although we both believed in the Holy Trinity and Jesus' sacrifice for our sins, our lives centered around each other instead of God. But obviously, I do not know what the last moments of Jim's life were like. Maybe he got on his knees and prayed. Maybe Jesus stood there in front of him (and everyone else) while the towers burned and asked: "Who do you say that I am?" ...and Jim answered correctly. Maybe it all happened so fast — and the next thing he knew, he was waiting in a line three-thousand people long to have his fate determined.

So I read Romans 3:22–24. "This righteousness from God comes through faith in Jesus Christ to all who believe. There is no difference, for all have sinned and fall short of the glory of God, and are justified freely by His grace through the redemption that came by Christ Jesus" (NIV).

I studied it. I meditated on it. I thought long and hard about it. And I found great comfort and peace in it. I believe in my heart that God erased Jim's sins from the chalkboard... the same way He helped me to erase those concerns from my mind...

·tf·

A cheerful heart is good medicine, but a crushed spirit dries up the bones.
~Proverbs 17:22 (NIV)

Chemistry

15

One day, a troubled woman at the counter asked to speak to a pharmacist, so I brought her into the private consultation area where she told me her dilemma. She wasn't asking for my professional advice — she just needed to vent her frustration. Her eight-year-old son was watching prime-time television when a commercial for Viagra came on. He innocently and inquisitively looked up at his mother and asked, "Mommy, what does *reptile... this... junction* mean?"

I sure wouldn't want to be the one to explain the meaning of "erectile dysfunction" to an eight-year-old. I'm glad it's not in my job description.

On another occasion, an elderly gentleman seemed anxious and asked to see the pharmacist. I went out to the counter, and he handed me a small, plastic, zip lock bag. Inside the bag was a single, round tablet. It appeared used and discolored, as if it had been through a washing machine. The frustrated man said, "These pills aren't working! I swallowed it whole, and it went right through me and came out again!" He had kindly brought me the evidence in the plastic bag.

Unfortunately, it *is* in my job description to explain that certain pills have a matrix core. The medicine diffuses out of the core leaving behind the shell, which passes through the body and is excreted in the stool. I did not want to know how or why this man retrieved the shell out of his stool, but he told me anyway — complete with graphic details. I'll spare you that part of the story.

As a practicing retail pharmacist for sixteen years, I have seen it all. (Then again, maybe there *is* more — a scary thought.) I am also very aware that patients do not like to leave the doctor's office without a prescription in their hands. That prescription gives them hope that soon they will feel better. And when they bring that piece of paper into the pharmacy and walk out with a little bottle of medicine, their hope becomes even stronger. We live in a society that believes taking a pill can fix almost any problem.

And more often than not, their medicine does indeed achieve the purpose it was prescribed for. The antibiotic killed the sinus infection. The nitroglycerin stopped the chest pain. The cream made the rash disappear. The painkiller eased the toothache.

And then there are the antidepressants. If you have read *A Tempered Faith*, consider this your refresher course with a spiritual twist. If not, you're about to get a short and simple lesson in pharmacology.

Antidepressants are used for many different psychiatric conditions, including (but not limited to) clinical depression and anxiety, which is a chemical imbalance of neurotransmitters in the brain. Unfortunately, there is no blood test to check the balance of the neurotransmitters in your brain, so diagnosis is made solely by recognizing the *symptoms* of clinical depression or anxiety: sadness, hopelessness, tiredness, restlessness, eating too much or too little, changes in sleep patterns, and losing interest in things you once enjoyed.

72

Hmmmm… that sounds exactly how I felt after losing Jim. In fact, that sounds like how we *all* feel at times, especially when we're stressed out. It would be nice if we could simply take a pill and watch those feelings of desperation just disappear.

But having those symptoms does *not* necessarily mean we all have clinical depression. There are other possible reasons for their existence: major lifestyle changes, a stressful event, the death of a loved one, the breakup of a marriage, the loss of income, even side effects from other medications. Keep in mind that if the chemicals in your brain are already normal, then taking these medications may shift your normal chemical balance into an abnormal state... which will make you feel even worse than before.

Please don't get me wrong. There are plenty of patients who have legitimately diagnosed mental illness. And there are plenty of medications that have tremendous value and benefit in treating the many forms of depression and anxiety. I've seen many patients who have been remarkably transformed and improved by these drugs. They were living in the pit of despair, and these medications have enabled them to once again enjoy their life and experience mental and emotional stability.

But also remember that the regimens are extremely individualized, and often it's a matter of trial and error until the doctor finds the right drugs and the right dosage for each patient. In my work, I have seen both ends of the spectrum and everything in between. I've seen many success stories, but I've also seen patients constantly struggling with their condition and discouraged by the side effects. Their doctors keep changing their medicine, the patients keep changing doctors, and sometimes the frustration of the whole experience adds to the anxiety and depression that they're trying to treat in the first place. Antidepressants are often misunderstood and over-prescribed; and all I'm saying is that one must evaluate the possible causes and understand the potential risks before one jumps on the antidepressant bandwagon.

I also believe we should recognize the benefits of using faith and pharmacy together by incorporating both medicinal healing

73

and spiritual healing into our lives. One treats our temporal condition, the other treats our eternal condition. There is a close relationship between our mental health, our physical health, and our spiritual health. God gives us the gifts of technology and the wisdom to continually develop new breakthroughs in medicine. But He also gives us so many other resources to draw from. He gives us His grace, His Word, His joy, His peace, and His promises. He gives us light in the darkness. He gives us strength when we are weak. He provides us with infinite forms of therapy that we can use together — to heal the body, the mind, and the soul.

It is common sense that when something breaks, we take it to the place it was made, or to an expert, to repair it. If your watch is broken, you don't take it to a plumber. If your car breaks down, you don't take it to the dentist. After 9/11, my heart was broken, and for a while, I took it to the drug store. I was swallowing handfuls of tranquilizers in the desperate attempt to numb my senses. But pills would not — *could not* — fix what was broken in my life. So I picked up the pieces of my shattered heart and I laid them at the feet of the One who created me in the first place... because He knew how my heart broke, and He knew exactly how to fix it. Which, by the way, would make God the Ultimate Cardiologist.

Faith and science have two common denominators: trust and hope. In the medical field, we trust in the healthcare provider's knowledge, experience, and accuracy. In the spiritual realm, we trust in the Savior's grace, mercy, and lovingkindness. In the medical field, a patient clings to hope for recovery. In the spiritual realm, Christians cling to hope for salvation. Religion and science are not always on opposite ends of the spectrum, as one might expect. Instead, they often run parallel to each other.

We visit the doctor for a physical checkup — but what about our spiritual checkup? We engage in preventative medicine for

74

our bodies — but what about for our souls? We take calcium supplements every day to strengthen our bones against osteoporosis — but how often do we read the Bible to strengthen our minds against the enemy? We run three miles a day on a treadmill to maintain our cardiovascular system — but how often do we pray to maintain our relationship with God? Preventative medicine should not be restricted to the doctor's office or the pharmacy. It should also be in our churches, in our homes, in our workplaces, in our schools, and in every facet of our lives.

Personally, I would much rather be under the influence of the Spirit of Christ than under the influence of mind-altering drugs. Instead of being dependent on tranquilizers, I'm proud to say that I'm dependent on God.

tf

A man's heart plans his way, but the LORD *directs his steps.*

~Proverbs 16:9 (NKJV)

Fire
Drill

16

The old, rugged cross on the cover of *A Tempered Faith* and *A Teachable Faith* is not simply a computer graphic. Nor is it the enormous cross of steel beams that still stands at Ground Zero. It is an eight-inch sculpture that was carved out of a steel girder from the World Trade Center and anonymously left for me at my church. It wasn't until *A Tempered Faith* was at the very last stage of publication — when the cases of books were ready to be shipped to the distributor — that we discovered who had sent me the cross. The compassionate and gifted carpenter of steel was Rich DePietro, and we wanted to acknowledge his kind gesture. So my publisher decided to print small postcards detailing the story of the cross and arranged to have the postcards placed into every book. This process took several weeks and threatened to delay the book's critical release date of September 11, 2003.

Of course, I became frantic as the release date approached and there were still no books available. I began to question my publisher's decision.

I can't believe this is taking so long! We've done a promotional blitz and orders have been placed —

what are we going to do if the books don't arrive
on time? Were those postcards really *necessary?*

Well, God knew they were necessary, and He made sure the job got done according to His divine schedule. And once again, God's timing was perfect. During the time when the postcards were being incorporated into the books at the printing facility, there was a devastating fire in the distributor's warehouse — where my books *would have been* had they been shipped according to the original schedule. Those postcards saved the entire inventory of my books. And in the end, neither the postcards nor the fire affected the book's release date.

It certainly humbled me and confirmed what I already knew to be true: I need to pray for God's will in my life and trust Him to work it out for His good purpose. He can see the whole picture. He can see around the corner — I can't.

In this particular case, my books were literally and divinely rescued from the flames. But sometimes, God metaphorically holds us directly in the fire. Isaiah 48:10 says, "See I have refined you, though not as silver; I have tested you in the furnace of affliction" (NIV). And Malachi 3:3 says, "He will sit as a smelter and purifier of silver... so that they may present to the LORD offerings in righteousness" (NASB).

The process of refining silver involves holding the metal in the center of a fire where the flames are the hottest to burn away all the impurities. The silversmith must constantly keep his eyes on the silver while it is in the fire, because if the silver is left even a moment too long in the flames, it will be destroyed. How does the silversmith know when the silver is fully refined? When he sees his image reflected in it.

It is certainly not pleasant when we are the ones in the middle of the fire, the heat is turned up, and the flames of sorrow and suffering scorch us. And God's silence and apparent with-drawal is not only frustrating, it's agonizing.

It reminds me of those one-way mirrors in police stations — where the cops can see the lineup, but the suspects cannot see the cops. We cannot see God, but His eyes are forever and al-ways upon us. As a silversmith, God will never remove us from His vision, even when we demand to know why He isn't remov-ing us from the fire. During the weeks when I impatiently waited for the postcards to be placed in the books, it felt like the heat was turned up and my plans would be burned. But the real blaze was tragically happening elsewhere, and only God could have known about it and intervened.

I'm sure you can think of an unpleasant occasion in your life when you squirmed in distress and wished to be relieved of it... but then looking back, you realized it was Providence and that it had happened for a good reason. There are vital lessons to be learned inside that fire... things that cannot be taught or learned within the borders of our own comfort zone.

tf

But no one can tame the tongue; it is a restless evil and full of deadly poison.
With it we bless our Lord and Father, and with it we curse men…
My brethren, these things ought not to be this way.

~James 3:8–10 (NASB)

Detention

17

My mother is the cutest little Italian lady and the best cook I know. Her tapioca pudding is a taste of heaven. Her meatballs have never been duplicated. Her brownies were always Jim's official birthday request and his prized possession. I could sell her homemade ravioli on eBay and get top dollar for them. From my earliest memories — and to this day — my mom has nursed me back to health, rejoiced in my triumphs, comforted my broken heart, guided me through major decisions, and fed me until I'm about to burst. So why would I ever yell at her?

"I do *not* have the time to figure out what's wrong with your computer, Mom. I have too much going on right now, and your problems are just gonna have to wait until next week." My tone was harsh. The tongue is a deadly poison. As soon as I said it, I wished I hadn't.

When life gets difficult, we tend to lash out at the people we care about the most. The two people who get to see my worst side are my poor mother and my boss (and dear friend), Rich. There was a third — but hopefully Jim is enjoying a much more peaceful life without me — which leaves my mother and Rich to take up the slack. Because of the constant support they give me, they rightfully deserve more respect — not less. And one would think that my awareness of this terrible habit would prevent me from further violations… but I keep blowing it… Fortunately for me, they are both masters at the art of forgiveness. As many times as my words and actions have hurt them, they're both willing to forget it and never look back.

If I could keep my behavior as neat as I keep my house, I'd be in good shape. My home is compulsively organized, since I am the sort of person who cannot think straight if things are awry. (In fact, before I sat down to write this chapter, I had to clean up my desk, line up my pens, and make sure the floor was vacuumed.) If only I was that obsessive about maintaining a good mood.

Moods are extremely contagious. It doesn't matter what kind of mood a person is in — good or bad — the "bug" can spread like wildfire to those around them. Mood bugs are airborne. They don't spread by direct contact — they spread like aerosol products sprayed in a small closet. Good moods, like air fresheners, can smell great — like a bakery or a new car. Soon the whole room is fragrant and everyone is smiling. Bad moods, like stink bombs, can smell nasty — like a skunk or a cesspool — and before long, everyone is running for the door.

If I was the CEO of a large corporation or even the owner of a small newspaper stand, I would surely want my employees to treat the customers with kindness and respect. After all, my staff represents my company, and my own reputation depends on how well I am represented. Have you ever shopped in a store where the cashier was so rude that you swore you'd never step foot in the place again? Yeah, me too. Yet there are many businesses that I continually return to, simply because the customer service excels over others. Rich has credited the success of his pharmacy to the pleasant nature of his employees who go the extra mile for the customers and have genuine concern for their needs.

Well, I'm not the CEO of a large corporation, nor am I a small business owner. I do, however, work for both. I still work a few hours a week for Rich at the pharmacy, but I also work full-time for God — the Creator of the universe and the CEO of the world. Both jobs require me to represent my boss to the best of my ability, and neither employer would want me setting off a rotten-attitude stink bomb or spreading a bad-mood bug around.

So would God have been impressed with the way I spoke to my poor mother? Of course not. That's certainly not how He would have handled it, and my mission as a Christian is to be like Him and to handle things His way. Unlike my retort to her plea for help, my mother's immediate forgiveness was truly Christ-like. She didn't even threaten to put soap in my mouth.

As Christians, we are "...ambassadors for Christ, as though God were making an appeal through us..." (2 Corinthians 5:20, NASB). Since my actions should reflect Him, they must make people want to go *to* Him — not turn people *away* from Him. My job is to demonstrate the love and kindness He gives so freely — not point them in the direction of the evil competitor. My job is to be a light in the darkness, the salt of the earth, a loyal soldier, a willing servant, a teachable student.

My job is to spread a good mood and to spread the Good News.

tf

Let your speech always be with grace, seasoned with salt, that you may know how you ought to answer each one.

~Colossians 4:6 (NKJV)

Pop
Quiz

18

On September 11,
2003, *A Tempered Faith* was nationally released and I was booked
for live interviews on several major television networks and syndicated radio programs, in recognition of the two-year anniversary of
the attacks. I had spent the one-year anniversary at Ground Zero;
it had been emotionally painful for me to be there, and I swore I
would never go back. But with the release of my book and the
scheduled media interviews, I had to return to the scene of the
crime. However, the interviews turned out to be a blessing, because
they not only gave me something positive to focus on — which
made the day pass quickly — but they also helped to spread my
message of overcoming tragedy through hope and faith in God.

I continue to do press, radio, and television interviews; and although there isn't anything too harsh or too personal that the
media hasn't asked me, it remains a strong vehicle for my ministry. I'll share with you some of the typical questions that I've
been asked...

Have you been able to forgive the terrorists?

The answer is yes. But keep in mind that I was never as angry
with the terrorists as I was with God... so God was the One I

needed to make my peace with, and clearly I have done that. Let me clarify that I am in no way defending or justifying what the terrorists did. It was incomprehensible, unjustifiable, and yes, to some, unforgivable.

I've also been asked what I would do if I were in a room with Osama Bin Laden. Just the two of us. Imagine that I'm sitting across a table from him, listening to him brag about his plans for the destruction of the towers. He has no remorse whatsoever. In fact, he talks about the September 11th attacks with pride and joy. I'm looking into the eyes of my husband's murderer, and I wonder what I would say to him or do to him…

I would like to think that I would behave righteously and honorably and that I wouldn't stoop to his level of disgrace. But I am human, and I do have human emotions. And as I think about that scenario, I wonder how Joseph *really* felt about his brothers when they sold him into slavery. Or how Daniel *really* felt about his co-workers when they threw him into the lion's den. Or how Mary *really* felt about Pilate and the crowd of people who were torturing and crucifying her Son. God's Son.

Joseph, Daniel, Mary, and countless others throughout history with similar stories were all human, and therefore they had normal human emotions: pain, fear, anguish, bitterness, resentment. Certainly they must have felt victimized, violated, betrayed, abandoned. How could they not?

But they also knew that the One who created them is also the One who will ultimately judge them. And the One who created their offenders is also the One who will ultimately judge their offenders. Deuteronomy 32:35 says, "Vengeance is Mine… in due time their foot will slip" (NASB). Mary might have been tempted to speed things up by throwing a banana peel in Pilate's path, but she patiently waited on God's promise.

And they also had a valuable gift called *restraint*. They all had the ability to stop themselves from doing or saying something that would have made a bad situation even worse. So I pray that if I ever find myself looking into the face of a terrorist, that I would recall Deuteronomy 32:35 and that I'd exercise that powerful, God-given gift of restraint. I also pray that justice will be served and that the terrorists will be sentenced for their crimes while they're still here on Earth. But should they be lucky enough to escape punishment in this world, I'm confident they will be condemned in the next.

During a recent secular TV interview, I answered that question, saying that I hoped I would behave righteously and honorably as a Christian. When the interview was over, the cameraman (let's call him Bob) said, "Jen, I have a very Christian response that you could use, if you're ever sitting at a table with Bin Laden."

I said, "Really? What is that?"

"Just tell him you're holding the seat for Bob. Then leave the room and come get me."

All humor aside, our society thinks in the mindset of payback. It's our human nature to retaliate when someone hurts us. But if we realize how much God has forgiven us, it becomes easier to forgive those who have hurt us. I think about what Joseph *could have done* to his brothers when they came to Egypt — starving and begging for food so many years after they had sold him into slavery and not recognizing that Joseph had become Egypt's ruler (Genesis chapter 45). An unforgiving reaction on Joseph's part would have literally changed the course of history forever. But instead, Joseph told his brothers, "As for you, you meant evil against me, but God meant it for good..." (Genesis 50:20, NASB).

Now *that's* what I would say to Osama Bin Laden if I ever

find myself face-to-face with him. Bitterness is the arsenic of the mind, and the antidote is the Sword of the Spirit.

How do you feel about the memorial design that was chosen for Ground Zero?

I have always strongly supported the efforts of preserving the footprints of the towers. That is sacred ground, and my opinion is that nothing other than a Memorial should be built on them. Once their preservation was secured — and at the time of this writing, we've been assured that is the case — then it really does not matter to me what style of a Memorial will be built on the site.

It is literally impossible to please three thousand families of victims and the entire city of New York. There is no single design that will make everyone happy. And quite honestly, there is no design that would have any personal significance for me.

We all grieve differently, and we all have our own individual ways of paying respect to our lost loved ones. Many families visit Ground Zero and find peace, comfort, and closure there, and I think it's wonderful that they are able to do so. I, for one, do not find peace at the site. As I wrote in *A Tempered Faith*, I prefer to remember Jim for the way he lived — *not* the way he died. Being at Ground Zero is far too much of a reminder to me of how he died — no matter how beautiful the Memorial design is.

What is your opinion about the situation in Iraq?

My heart breaks for the families of the American soldiers who have been lost in the Middle East and for the troops who continue to diligently fight and risk their lives. I pray for them every day.

I believe that it is crucial that we — as a nation — investigate what could have or should have been done to prevent the 9/11 attacks, because certainly we need to learn from our past in order to protect our future. I believe we should find the problem, fix it — not dwell on it — and move on.

Whether or not the U.S. should be involved with the war in the Middle East? I do not have an opinion on that issue — it is a politically complicated subject about which I am not wise enough to give an answer. My mission is not to cast blame on our government for security issues or to develop political opinions about the situation in the Middle East. There are plenty of people far more qualified than I to do that. My mission is to continue to heal, to keep moving forward, and to glorify God and His Kingdom.

In A Tempered Faith, *you were very adamant against forming any new romantic relationships. Do you still feel that way?*

I have absolutely *no* intention whatsoever of remarrying, nor do I have any intention whatsoever of even beginning a new romance. My love for Jim is still so intense and I cannot imagine being with anyone else.

That being said, however, I also had absolutely no intention whatsoever of becoming a widow — at that age, in that way. I cannot predict my future any better now than I could have before 9/11. The only thing I do know for sure: if God wants another man in my life, He'll make it happen. And that's all I have to say about that.

tf

"For My thoughts are not your thoughts, nor are your ways My ways," declares the LORD. *"For as the heavens are higher than the earth, so are My ways higher than your ways and My thoughts than your thoughts."*

~Isaiah 55:8–9 (NASB)

Lost and Found

19

The third anniversary of losing Jim passed as quickly as the second and I thank God for taking my hand and walking me through it. On that day — September 11, 2004 — I had two speaking engagements in my hometown. I was relieved that I didn't have to go to Ground Zero again (whew!), but God still used the challenges of the day to take me out of my comfort zone and grow me up just a little bit more.

This was the first time I was scheduled to speak twice on the same day at completely different venues and using different programs. (Of course, God chose my most emotionally difficult day of the year to accomplish that.) It was also the first time I would be speaking outdoors — one of the events was a 9/11 Remembrance Service on the beach. During that program, I had to learn to contend with nature. It was a sunny but very windy day, and twice my notes almost blew away while I was speaking (I had a flashback to my brother's piano concert and his airborne sheet music). There were also large, buzzing, stinging insects flying around my head while I spoke. A racing powerboat sped by in the water, and a loud, low-flying military aircraft flew overhead. Distractions are my greatest downfall, but I've become teachable. I've learned that when I can't control them myself, I simply have to ask God to help me deal with them.

But on that day, God had a whole lot more to teach me about the uncontrollable forces of nature.

For those of you who have not read *A Tempered Faith*, I must briefly tell you about one of the amazing tributes to Jim after 9/11. Jim and I were avid scuba divers, and one of our favorite places to dive was Grand Cayman, a small island in the Caribbean. In May of 2002, after many deliberations with Cayman's Department of Environment and agreement to the strict marine preservation laws, a bronze memorial plaque was placed underwater on a coral reef in Jim's memory. A new mooring was built, and a new dive site was born. It is called Jim Sands Memorial Reef, and it is the most incredible tribute to Jim. I cannot imagine a more perfect way to honor him, and I'm quite sure he'd agree with me.

But remember those uncontrollable forces of nature I was talking about? The 2004 hurricane season was one of the most devastating in history. Charley, Frances, Ivan, and Jeanne wreaked havoc in the southern states and on many islands in the Caribbean. Lives were lost, countless people were left homeless, and the damage was catastrophic.

Little did I know as I addressed the crowd at the windy, outdoor 9/11 Remembrance Service, that the island of Grand Cayman was taking a direct hit from Hurricane Ivan at that precise time. It was a disastrous Category 5 storm that caused massive destruction both topside and underwater.

Jim's memorial plaque has not been seen since.

The absolute irony, of course, is that I lost Jim on September 11, 2001, and three years later *to the day*, I lost his memorial. Both of them were gone in a single day of tragedy, and neither of them will ever be recovered.

And I confess that, for a brief time, I went back to my old, bad habits. I once again questioned God, although certainly not with the bitterness that I had four years ago.

> *Why do You allow these things to happen? You can say that 9/11 was an act of free will by mankind… but what about hurricanes? Tornados? Earthquakes? That's not free will — they're natural disasters — and I know You are a sovereign God and You can stop these things from happening if You choose to… So why don't You choose to? People have lost their lives, their homes, their jobs, their incomes, every certainty they thought they had. I know it pales in comparison, but I have once again lost something very dear to me, so* WHY?

And He answered me with Deuteronomy 29:29. "The secret things belong to the LORD…" (NASB).

> *Okay, Lord, okay. I won't ask why. I know You're going to explain it to me one day. And I know that by questioning You, it implies that I don't trust You, and that's not the case. And I also know that there are countless evils and dangers that you do protect us from every day, and we aren't even aware of it. So I won't ask why. Instead, I'll ask* what. *What are you trying to teach me from this?*

And He answered me again — this time with 2 Corinthians 4:18. "While we look not at the things which are seen, but at the things which are not seen; for the things which are seen are temporal, but the things which are not seen are eternal" (NASB).

> *Okay, Lord, I get it. It's a material thing. I can't take Jim's memorial plaque with me when I leave this planet. I need to keep a tight grip on the one thing I should be holding onto — Your hand. If I ever let go of Your hand, I'm on my own. And that's one place I do not want to be.*

I am grateful to God for providing this tribute to honor Jim in the first place. I am grateful for the opportunity to have seen the plaque underwater during the dedication of Jim's reef and to have a spectacular video of the dive, which so beautifully captures the memory of it. And I am grateful that for two years, many divers were able to see the plaque and to remember Jim's life.

God has a way of using tragedies to bring us closer to Him. Sometimes, that's what it takes to get our attention and to remind us to cherish each day. Sometimes, that's what it takes to make us teachable.

·ℐ·

In God, whose word I praise, in God I trust; I will not be afraid. What can mortal man do to me?

~Psalm 56:4 (NIV)

Civics

20

I got the phone call on the Thursday afternoon of August 12, 2004. It was my publisher calling from Georgia, sounding a bit concerned. "Jen, *what* is going on up there in New Jersey?"

Since I hadn't been watching the news, I did not know what he was talking about, but he proceeded to tell me. New Jersey Governor James McGreevey had just made a shocking announcement on national television with his wife and family standing at his side: he is a gay American and had a homosexual affair with a former employee.

My stomach did a few cartwheels, and I broke out into a hot sweat. Governor McGreevey had written the Foreword to *A Tempered Faith* more than a year before in the summer of 2003. When he read my manuscript and agreed to write the Foreword, I was thrilled and honored that he considered my story good enough to endorse my book. His foreword was beautifully written, and I was (and still am) grateful for his kind words. I received endorsements from other political, religious, and literary leaders, but Governor McGreevey's name was chosen to appear under mine on the cover of the book's dust jacket. One year later, that decision proved to be perilous.

All opinions of McGreevey's lifestyle aside — political, moral,

97

or otherwise — the fact is this: anything that diverts attention away from the message of a book is not a good thing. And so the appearance of a controversial figure's name on the cover of my book could overpower my testimony with potentially disastrous consequences.

After McGreevey's announcement, our distributor contacted my publisher and said, "We cannot sell this book — it's *the kiss of death*." The kiss of death?! I was horrified. For me, this has never been — nor will it ever be — about money or book sales or royalties. This is about spreading a powerful message of overcoming adversity in our lives through obedience and trust in God, and I consider anything that potentially hinders that message to be a direct attack from the enemy in an attempt to shut down my operation. The closer we follow God, the greater a threat we are to the evil one. But I will not be defeated — I belong to the team that has already won. God is calling the shots here, and the outcome is *always* His.

So I went into full-scale spiritual warfare mode.

I prayed about it. I prayed for my book. I prayed for the people who considered buying it and/or reading it — especially if they have a negative opinion of McGreevey. I prayed that they would not blindly overlook the value of what is inside. I prayed for Governor McGreevey. I prayed for his family to find strength and courage in dealing with his choices. I prayed for my own peace of mind and that God would help me to accept whatever lay ahead. I actually lost sleep over this ridiculous mess, I had so much anxiety. So I looked for comfort in the Scriptures, and I found it. "Be anxious for nothing, but in everything by prayer... let your requests be made known to God" (Philippians 4:6, NKJV).

I looked a little deeper and found more. "Cast your burden upon the LORD and He will sustain you" (Psalm 55:22, NASB).

Wow, I had hit a gold mine. "Trust in the LORD with all your heart and do not lean on your own understanding. In all your ways acknowledge Him, and He will make your paths straight" (Proverbs 3:5–6, NASB). I slept well that night.

I had to accept that since there was very little we could do with regard to damage control for the book, it would all come down to laying it at God's feet and trusting Him to direct my paths... and He did. Before long, the New Jersey governor scandal was no longer front page news and our distributor was no longer referring to *A Tempered Faith* as the "kiss of death."

Oh, and I decided I would not ask political figures to endorse any future books.

tf

Jesus answered them, "Destroy this temple, and I will raise it again in three days."

~John 2:19 (NIV)

Class
Bully

21

I recently gave my outdated kitchen a well-needed facelift. The old, stained linoleum was replaced with porcelain floor tile. Down with the rickety pressboard cabinets; up with traditional cherry wood cupboards. Gone is the 1980s wallpaper and coordinating Pepto Bismol-pink backsplash; in its place are rich, neutral earth tones with just a hint of a grapevine theme.

While the kitchen renovation was taking place, I thought about how God is the Divine Architect and Interior Designer. He has the blueprints of our lives — we don't. God is in the business of renovation (I suppose those years as a carpenter didn't hurt), and fortunately for us, He doesn't work by the rules of *Trading Spaces* (one weekend to finish and a budget of $1,000).

Sometimes He'll simply throw a fresh coat of paint on our lives, and we love when He does that, right? A job promotion, a newborn grandchild, a clean bill of health. Other times, He's knocking down walls, like He did with me. But I have full confidence that in the end, all of this demolition in my life will all be worthwhile... because God knows what He's doing.

A few months ago, I was preparing dinner for several guests. I looked out of my new kitchen window and to my horror saw that a spider on steroids had made an enormous web outside, using each corner of the window's frame as the web's anchor. The web literally stretched over the entire length and width of the window pane (thirty inches long by twelve inches wide — I measured it), and the enormous spider, which resembled a Mallomar with eight legs, was sitting in the center of the web. I screamed, dropped my spatula, and ran for cover. [Author Note: For those of you who are not from the mid-Atlantic region and therefore may not be familiar with Mallomars–they are round graham cracker cookies topped with a big dollop of marshmallow and covered in chocolate, and they bring unbridled joy to those of us who consume them.]

Now please understand. I suffer from serious arachnophobia and insectophobia of every species — crawling, flying, hopping, and stinging. In whatever form they are, bugs and I do not cohabitate. They are strictly prohibited from entering my home. And if they should successfully find their way inside, they will pay for it with their lives — death by vacuum. Although this particular spider was in his own authorized territory, he was big and ugly and an unsightly disturbance of the view from my beautiful new window. My dinner guests would be arriving shortly, and since this was the first time they would be seeing my newly renovated kitchen, I did not want a tarantula to be part of the décor.

Of course, this one's way down at the bottom on the list of significance, but it's just one of a billion reasons why I miss Jim so much: he was my officially authorized bug exterminator. There have been many times since 9/11 when I frantically chased after a cricket in my living room as it leaped over end tables and vaulted over ottomans, and all the while I was bawling because Jim wasn't around to kill it for me. But I have since accepted the fact that if I want the occasional insect removed from my house, I have to do it myself. Ugh.

Back to the spider on steroids. I'm sure there are some of you who are disturbed and upset by my plot to remove an innocent creature that has made its home in the confines of nature. But notice I said *remove* it, not *kill* it. I do have some mercy, thank you very much. I decided to spare his life and simply eliminate his residence. Armed with a long-handled broom, I bravely went outside and approached the behemoth and his web. I made as much noise as I could so he would sense me coming — which he did. He scurried away from his web and took refuge under a loose shingle on the house. That made it easy for me — I took the broom and brushed away every single strand of the massive web, leaving no evidence of it whatsoever. I have to admit I had a slight pang of guilt at leaving the spider homeless — but that quickly passed when my dinner guests raved over the kitchen and admired the beautiful view outside the clean, webless window. Besides, I thought, the spider will be perfectly happy in his new home under the loose shingle. I'll even let him stay there as long as he wants.

The next morning, I got out of bed and dragged myself into the kitchen to make a cup of tea. I glanced out the window and couldn't believe my eyes — I thought maybe I was hallucinating, but no, there it was. The spider was back, complete with a brand new web in the same exact spot on the window. Maybe it was my imagination, but this web seemed even larger and more intricate than the one I had destroyed the day before. With my mouth hanging open in disbelief, I examined it closely through the window, half expecting to see "NICE TRY" weaved among the threads. And the Mallomar with eight legs once again sat in the very center, no doubt exhausted after a very busy and productive night. I decided it was a *she*, not a *he*, named her Charlotte, and invited her to stay.

I made my cup of tea, sat at my kitchen counter, and stared

in amazement at Charlotte's creation. Even more astounding is the fact that God even gives spiders the ability to rebuild their lives after a devastating loss. Charlotte's whole world — as she knew it — was completely and utterly demolished by me... which, incidentally, makes me a *terrorist* in the arachnid world (talk about the paradox of role reversal). Yet in a matter of hours, she was able to spin a new home and move on with her life. If God can equip a spider to accomplish such a feat, how much more will He enable us to overcome any disaster?!

I realized more clearly than ever that God had given me everything I need to survive the tragedy of 9/11 and rebuild my life after the dust settled. Unlike the spider, I had a lot of help and quite a few resources to draw from. Through Charlotte, I learned the truth of 2 Corinthians 9:8. "And God is able to make all grace abound to you, so that in all things at all times, having all that you need, you will abound in every good work" (NIV). God wants to reveal His will to us. He desires for us to see a glimpse of the blueprints of our futures. He longs for us to follow His plans, because His plans for our lives are far better than anything we could ever design for ourselves. So often we meet Him with resistance, especially when the unthinkable happens and we cannot possibly grasp that His way is truly better. And since God gave us the ability to make choices, we sometimes choose our way over His. But if we do that, our web will never get rebuilt, and we will continue to live in fear and darkness, never really moving out from behind that loose shingle, never discovering the exciting things that God has up His sleeve for us.

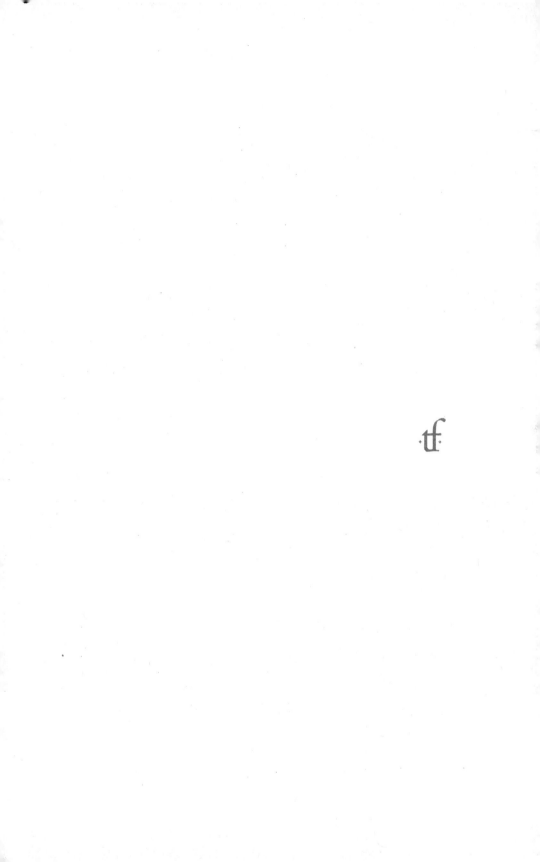

They see the works of the LORD, and His wonders in the deep.

~Psalm 107:24 (NKJV)

Recess

22

Jim and I never missed an opportunity to dive, explore the underwater world, and marvel at its splendor. Jim also enjoyed underwater photography, and he truly had a gift for capturing the beauty of marine life on film. We were fascinated with every fish and creature — no matter how big or small, no matter how common or rare. We loved to study marine identification books, because we wanted to become familiar with all the fish, their habitats, their behavior, and their stages of life. It made diving even more enjoyable when we recognized the fish, knew what to expect from them, and anticipated how they would react to us.

We were always amazed at how much activity there is on a single reef. Everywhere we turned, the busy underwater world was happening right in front of us like Manhattan at rush hour. Despite the boundless energy around the reef and so much to see, we considered diving to be truly relaxing. Jim used to say it was the ultimate form of stress therapy. I said it was like heroin — addictive, and it wasn't long before you needed another fix.

Jim had a way with fish — they trusted him. His motions were always slow and gentle, never threatening. He not only had the required patience for photography, but he had perfect neutral buoyancy. Jim had a natural ability to fine-tune his breathing so he could literally stay motionless, waiting patiently for that gold-entail moray eel to pop its head out of the hole in the coral so he could get the perfect shot. Sometimes Jim would hover completely upside down and perfectly still with his head just above the sandy bottom to photograph a lobster hiding under a coral ledge. Or he'd get incredibly close to a stingray partially buried in the sand without disturbing it at all.

I miss diving terribly, and I miss my dive buddy even more. Yet as I reminisce about our underwater experiences, I see some parallels between my old life and my new life...

Back then, I studied books to become familiar with marine life. Now, I study the Bible to become familiar with the Creator of that marine life.

Back then, I relied on the buddy system, a compass for navigation, and life support equipment to compensate for buoyancy and pressure. Now, I still have a buddy system — I rely on God for navigation and life support, and He gives me all the resources I need to compensate for life's pressures.

Back then, I knew that staying physically fit and maintaining my dive skills would play a critical role in solving problems underwater. Now, I know that staying spiritually fit and maintaining my trust and obedience in God will play a critical role in solving problems in my life.

Scuba diving requires skilled training for the potential hazards and risks underwater. Anything can happen down there: a diver can run out of air, become entangled in fishing line, get caught in a strong current, or become separated from his dive buddy. Following proper procedures can mean the difference between life or death. If a diver gets into trouble underwater, one of the cardinal rules is this: stop, think, and act.

- STOP all activity, relax, and remain calm. Do not panic.

- THINK about your options and use your experience and knowledge to quickly determine the best course of action to take. Do not panic.

- ACT intelligently and apply the necessary skills you've learned. Do not panic.

The journey of life also requires special training to survive a crisis. And when we encounter one, we can use the same rule that scuba divers do: stop, think, and act.

- STOP, relax, remain calm, and do not panic. Remember Ecclesiastes 10:4. "Calmness can lay great errors to rest" (NIV).

- THINK about your options and use the wisdom and resources that God has provided to determine the best course of action. Pray for clarity of mind and God's guidance and direction. Do not panic. Remember 1 Kings 22:5. "'First seek the counsel of the LORD'" (NIV).

- ACT intelligently and apply the Word of God to the circumstances in your life. Do not panic. Remember James 1:22. "But be doers of the word, and not hearers only" (NKJV).

So God used the underwater skills that I learned many years ago, and He taught me to apply them to my problems topside. He's always preparing us. He's always equipping us. He's always at work.

After 9/11, Jim's story and some of his underwater photos appeared in his favorite dive magazine, Rodale's *Scuba Diving*. Not only did that amazing tribute lead to my new career as a writer/speaker and the publication of my books, but it also brought about another special way to remember Jim. The magazine article caught the eye of Peter E. Marck, the producer of an underwater/diving cable TV series in Boston. Peter eventually formed the organization of UETC (Underwater Education and Training Center) in Boston, and this is an excerpt from UETC's September, 2004 newsletter:

> *I never knew Jim, but I read an article about him in* Scuba Diving *magazine in March 2002 and never forgot about him. We planned to develop a scholarship program for* UETC, *and I felt a strong conviction to name our scholarship in Jim's memory. I began to search for Jim's wife, Jennifer Sands, to seek her approval for putting my idea into action. I successfully found her through the miracle of the Internet, and Jennifer gave her blessing on this project. I also discovered that Jim had earned a degree in biology with an intention to pursue marine biology — until his career took a detour into the computer industry. How very appropriate that we will pay tribute to Jim, with the establishment of the Jim Sands Memorial Marine Education Scholarship, by helping others to learn about marine science — something that Jim had always enjoyed and endeavored.*

This scholarship holds a special place in my heart. Amazingly, it came to fruition just weeks after Jim's memorial in Grand Cayman had been lost — as if God replaced one tribute with another. But I also saw how God can teach us in the most indirect and unassuming ways. Because of 9/11, I have received an education in overcoming trials through faith in my Creator. And because of 9/11, two students will receive a scholarship for education in marine sciences orchestrated by the Creator of marine life Himself. Whether on land or at sea, we are all students in this classroom of life.

tf

The sins of some men are obvious, reaching the place of judgment ahead of them; the sins of others trail behind them.

~1 Timothy 5:24 (NIV)

Driver's Ed

23

It was November of 1998, and Jim and I had just leased a brand new silver Jeep Grand Cherokee Limited with a 5.9-liter engine. It had power, style, luxury, comfort, and we were very excited about it.

Soon after we got it, Jim drove our new pride and joy to work for the first time — a brutal, two-hour commute on the Garden State Parkway and the New Jersey Turnpike. Both roads are superhighways with heavy traffic. As he was driving home late one evening, his pride was humbled. Oh, how I wish Jim was here to tell this story in his own entertaining words...

He was driving about 65–70 miles an hour in the center lane, several car lengths behind the car in front of him. Suddenly, the car ahead swerved to avoid an object in the road. Jim then saw that the object was actually an old mattress — it was in his lane directly in his path. There were cars on either side of Jim, so he could not swerve to avoid it. He held his breath and said to himself, "Let's see how this SUV handles bumps!" Then he drove right over the mattress. He was impressed with how well the Jeep rolled right over it with barely a thump... and he was impressed with his own decisive control of the situation. Apparently, other drivers were impressed with the truck and Jim's skills as well, since there were many wide-eyed glances from the occupants of passing cars. He grinned smugly and thought to himself, *Yup, this is my new* SUV. *Pretty nice, huh? And it handles like a dream.*

A little while later, he came to a tollbooth. As he pulled into the cash lane, the attendant looked at Jim — and with a tinge of sarcasm — said, "Excuse me, sir, but are you aware that there's a mattress stuck to the back of your vehicle?"

And so, my poor, mortified husband held up traffic at the tollbooth as he pulled over to the side of the road with his sad mattress tagging along. Upon closer inspection, Jim concluded that when he drove over the mattress, it must have bounced up and impaled itself onto the vehicle's sharp tow hook. He had been driving like that for over five miles.

Humiliated, Jim pulled the mattress off the tow hook and left it on the side of the road. Now the occupants of passing cars were shooting glances of disdain at him, as if to say, "Hey buddy, why don't you dump your garbage in your own back yard and stop polluting the environment?"

I remember how embarrassed I was years before when I left the ladies room in a restaurant with a piece of toilet paper stuck to the bottom of my shoe. (Tell me what woman hasn't had that happen to her!) So with empathy and compassion, I tried to comfort poor Jim, telling him that he did a good deed. After all, he had removed dangerous debris from the road, thereby averting a potentially hazardous situation for other vehicles... right? It didn't work. As a result of the incident, Jim's new car excitement level plummeted, and it was never fully restored. We eventually traded in the Jeep for a simple, tow hookless Nissan Maxima.

How often do we go through life dragging things around that we're not even aware of? What kind of unnecessary cargo do we carry with us on our journey? What are the burdens of our past and present that weigh us down and threaten our future? It's not about a piece of toilet paper stuck to the bottom of our shoe...

114

or a mattress stuck to the back of our car. It's about our attitude and our behavior, our thoughts and words and actions, our bad habits, our unhealthy obsessions, our unclean conscience.

Whenever I see a Jeep, I can't help but think of Jim's mattress story. After I get done laughing, I ask God to reveal to me what kind of ugly, old mattresses that *I'm* dragging around with me. Since there are an abundance of Jeeps on the road, I've had plenty of opportunities to do some soul searching. I'll share with you what I've come up with so far.

I'm still dragging *worry* and *anxiety* around with me. Why do I worry about things when I know without a shadow of a doubt that God is in total control of this world and of my life? Why am I anxious about things that I cannot control? Jesus Himself told us, "Do not worry... but seek first His kingdom and His righteousness, and all these things will be added to you. So do not worry about tomorrow; for tomorrow will care for itself" (Matthew 6:31–34, NASB).

I'm still dragging around a *stubborn streak* and a *hot temper*. James chapter three tells us, "And the tongue is a fire... from the same mouth come both blessing and cursing" (NASB). Make that a Sicilian tongue and I'm really in trouble.

I'm still dragging *guilt* around with me. There are far too many things I've done in my past that I'm not proud of. I told God about them (even though He already knew), and I told Him how sorry I was. He dropped the case and never looked back. I'm the one who keeps bringing them up — like a torture device. It is then that I must recall Romans 8:39: "... [nothing] will be able to separate us from the love of God..." (NASB).

I'm still dragging around *impatience*. Working with cranky customers at the pharmacy would be a test of patience for anyone — and I admit I've often failed that test — but the circumstances are no excuse. So if I've been on hold with an insurance company for twenty minutes trying to work out an issue for a customer, and that customer becomes agitated *with me* because it's taking so long, how should I react to him? "For what credit is there if, when you sin and are harshly treated, you endure it with patience? But if when you do what is right and suffer for it you patiently endure it, this finds favor with God" (1 Peter 2:20, NASB).

Sometimes the mattress of transgression that I drag around in my life is like a king-size waterbed, and I can feel its weight as I pull it along behind me. Other times, it's more inconspicuous — like an inflatable pillow — and it might even go unnoticed until God makes me aware of it...

Either way, I still need to learn how to abandon it along the side of the road.

·tf·

Consequently, you are no longer foreigners and aliens, but fellow citizens with God's people and members of God's household.

~Ephesians 2:19 (NIV)

Field
Trip

24

"God bless America!"

Those were my father's bellowing, emphatic words as the plane touched down at Newark Airport following our family's exciting-but-exhausting, two-week tour of Italy during the summer of 2004. He had experienced a few disappointments. First of all, we didn't visit any golf courses. Then he discovered that there was no Folgers decaf — only hair-curling espresso. Then, in Tuscany, he almost broke his teeth on the bread, which is hard as concrete because of the water they use to make it. Throughout the next two weeks, we would inevitably hear Dad singing *God Bless America* at random intervals. I must admit I joined in on the chorus a few times, like when I discovered some unconventional — and female unfriendly — toilets in some of the restaurants.

In spite of the culture shock, we all had a blast. There were seven of us traveling abroad together: Mom, age seventy-four, who walks with a steel rod in her right femur from a broken leg two years ago — amazingly, she kept up with us on those steep, cobblestone roads in Florence; Dad, age seventy-six, who jogs on a treadmill and does thirty, military-style pushups (I can't even do five) every morning, and therefore *we* had to keep up with *him*; Maria and Tom, who had toured Italy a few years before;

their sons Kevin (who once spent an entire summer there) and Brian (his first time); and yours truly.

We spent the first week in the northern Tuscany region, where the breathtaking landscapes of vineyards and olive groves are magnificent. We took a tour of a vineyard and an olive press in Siena to see how wine and olive oil are made. We left with minds full of knowledge and stomachs full of rock-hard bread dipped in delicious oil.

I learned that it takes an olive tree thirty years to mature and that its cultivation requires peaceful conditions. Ripe olives are hand picked from the tree and placed in an olive press, which squeezes oil from the olives. This process requires the olives to go through extreme conditions, but the resulting oil has great value and multiple purposes.

Hey, that sounds strangely familiar. It took *me* about thirty years to spiritually grow to this level, and it only happened once I found that peaceful condition through Christ, who never left me while I was being pressed and squeezed. And Christ Himself was being pressed and squeezed in the Garden of Gethsemane (which, by the way, means *oil press* in Hebrew), as He agonized over the suffering He was about to endure…

I will never look at an olive the same way again.

✦ ✦ ✦

I fell in love with Rome and its art and history and culture and ancient ruins and normal toilets and great gelato. One of the highlights of my trip was visiting the jail cell where the apostles Paul and Peter were imprisoned two thousand years ago. As I stood in the small, cold, dark dungeon, I imagined how awful it must have been for them. And yet, while Paul was being held captive by the Romans in that dreadful chamber, he wrote to the Philippians, "...I have learned to be content in whatever circumstances I am... I have learned the secret of being filled and going hungry, both of having abundance and suffering need. I can do all things through Him who strengthens me" (Philippians 4:11–13, NASB). If that didn't humble me and put my life into perspective, I don't know what will.

Speaking of humility, using the restrooms in remote areas of Italy was quite an adventure — you never knew what you were going to find. We encountered several porcelain "holes in the floor" throughout our travels. This may be acceptable for men, but for ladies, it is virtually impossible to use. Some toilets actually had a place to sit, but the seat was on a tight spring set in the "up" position, which required the female user to be a contortionist in order to hold it down and sit on it. If you stood up too fast, the seat would spring back up — boinnnggg!! My poor mother limped out of one public restroom in Pisa with a look of terror on her face. And we wonder why that tower leans.

Our biggest challenge in Italy was driving to stay alive. We rented an oversized van that Tom drove, and he handled it exceptionally well, considering there are basically no rules or speed limits. Stop signs are optional and red lights are more like... suggestions. Dad promised he would never complain about the bad drivers in New Jersey again.

I did an unscheduled speaking engagement outside of Naples at a church led by American missionaries (and friends of our family), Tim and Marcia Monahan. At their request, I gave my testimony for their congregation while Pastor Monahan translated my words into Italian. We were told that many citizens of Italy are very disconnected to the global significance of 9/11, and they hoped my story would also help the congregation to deal with their own life struggles.

I spoke about my life before and after that tragic day and how I have found peace and strength through Christ. God enabled my testimony to personalize 9/11 — it made the tragedy real for them. When I was finished, a few members of the congregation approached me. One gentleman held my hands, and with tears in his eyes, he spoke from his heart while his friend translated in broken English. "On 9/11, I was so angry at the men who did this. But that was a long time ago and I forgot about it. Now I hear you, and now I am angry all over again, because I see how you and America have suffered."

A young man and his wife made a successful attempt at communicating their feelings in English. "We did not really think about 9/11 very much, because no one ever talks about it here. It just wasn't important to us — until now. We are going through some hard times ourselves, but if you can get through 9/11, we can get through our problems."

But the one who brought tears to my eyes was the sweet, little, Italian lady dressed in black. She asked someone to translate for her. "You donna know me and I donna know you, but I praya for you on nina-elev and my prayers were answered 'causa heera you are."

Grazie, Gesù... grazie. Thank You, Jesus... thank You.

...to bestow on them a crown of beauty instead of ashes, the oil of gladness instead of mourning, and a garment of praise instead of a spirit of despair.
~Isaiah 61:3, (NIV)

Dress Code

25

It was only my second date with this guy, Jim Sands, and I knew he would be arriving at my house in a few minutes. I had just enough time to run upstairs and grab a sweater from my closet.

I reached up and pulled the hanger off the rack. I heard a strange popping noise, then CRASH! — the entire clothes rack had come off the wall. It fell on top of me, and I was buried underneath a heavy pile of clothes. That's when the doorbell rang.

Oh, no, I can't believe this. Not now! I had to swim to the surface, untangling myself from pant legs, peeling silk blouses off my head, and tossing belts out of the way. It seemed like an eternity before I could pull myself out of the closet, and I was afraid that Jim would give up and go home. I ran downstairs, even though my hair was now a mess and I looked like Who-Did-It-And-Ran.

"Hang on! I'm coming!" I yelled, hoping he was even still there.

In my frantic rush down the stairs, I smacked my hand on a sharp edge of the wooden banister. It took a chunk out of my knuckle, and now I was bleeding. *Ow! This is just great!* I grabbed a tissue from the bathroom on my mad dash to the front door.

"I'm sorry! Just one more second!" I was sure he was gone by now.

I got to the door, reached for the doorknob, turned it, and pulled. The door did not open. I pulled harder. That's when the doorknob came off in my hands.

I heard Jim laughing on the other side of the door. *The good news is, he's still here. The bad news is, when he sees what I look like, he'll wish he wasn't.* I let him in through the garage, and even though I was bleeding, frazzled, and closely resembled Roseanne Rosanna-Danna, he graciously took me out to dinner anyway. He even fixed my closet and my doorknob.

I've become a much stronger person since 9/11, but there are still some things I don't have the emotional strength to do. I still can't go into Jim's closet or his dresser drawers. I'm just not there yet. In many other areas of my life, God has me on the fast forward track — but not with Jim's closet. I'm stuck on pause. There's a part of me that just wants to preserve things the way they were before. I'm confident that the day will come when I find the courage, strength, and desire to go through Jim's clothes — and it will be a bittersweet day, indeed — until then, they'll stay status quo.

As for my own now-steel-reinforced closet. A few months ago, I got into one of those moods to clear things out, so I undertook a purging of my clothes, which soon led to a confrontation with reality: too many of them didn't fit anymore. I'd been avoiding this task for years — call it denial, call it laziness, call it wishful thinking — but the time had come, and the used clothing bins were bulging by the time I got done with them.

It was a tiring project, but I learned a lot. I noticed how consistently I was drawn to black and pink. I realized that I owned clothes I had never worn even once but had refused to part with, simply because I *might* wear them one day. I saw that some of the clothes had been hanging in my closet for so long that the style had gone out of fashion and come back in again. I never thought of myself as a pack rat — but after that archaeological excavation, I realized how much I had squirreled away over the years.

God used my overstuffed closet to teach me a few things. He revealed many of my own heart issues and struggles, my own idols and false worship, and He made me aware of other areas of my life that need purging. I realized that since I am "a new creation; the old has gone, the new has come" (2 Corinthians 5:17, NIV), many things in my old life do not fit me anymore. So I made room in the closet of my new life for God.

I started with my language. "Oh my God" is no longer a frequent impulsive part of my speech (as in "Oh my God, I broke a nail" or "Oh my God, can you believe it?"). God longs for us to address Him — but we need to do it with the respect and sincerity He so rightly deserves, and we need to reserve "Oh my God" for our heartfelt prayers to Him. There are other unfavorable words that no longer fit my new life, and I've removed them from my vocabulary as well.

Next was television. Gone from my routine is *The Today Show*, and in its place are my morning devotionals and Bible readings. Gone is *Late Night with David Letterman*, and in its place are my writings to God in my prayer journal. Now please understand: I'm not saying that God frowns upon television or those particular shows. But my days are very busy and my time is very limited, and therefore I need to prioritize my life. For whatever reason, God created only twenty-four hours in a day (can't wait to hear His rationale for that one), and I made a commitment to spend more time with Him, so something had to go. Sorry, Katie and Matt. Sorry, David.

The old Meat Loaf *Bat out of Hell* CD in my car has taken a back seat to Steven Curtis Chapman. Again, I'm not implying that God has something against the music of Meat Loaf (then again, He might). But I simply prefer to listen to music that fits my new life. Pat Benatar has been replaced by Amy Grant. Aerosmith has been replaced by Avalon. The Rolling Stones have been replaced by *WOW Hits 2003*. I think you get the idea.

When I committed my life to Christ, my attitude and behavior changed, because God changed my heart. I no longer desire to please myself but to please Him. I have lost interest in conforming to the styles of world — I only want to conform to the fashion of His will. In one single day of tragedy, the entire wardrobe of my life was changed, and God is now in total control of it. So I won't squeeze Him into my closet, squished among all the other garments of my life. I will continue to make spacious room for Him, and He will continue to clothe me with the warmth of His love... kind of like that comfortable, old, flannel shirt that I refuse to give away.

Before his downfall a man's heart is proud, but humility comes before honor.
~Proverbs 18:12 (NIV)

The Dog Ate My Homework

26

At two years post-9/11, the newness of my life was quite overwhelming. I was still adjusting to life without Jim (still am, always will be). I was still adjusting to my new and improved relationship with God. I was a new (first-time) author without previous knowledge or experience in the publishing industry. And I was a new speaker, having never spoken to audiences before *A Tempered Faith* was released. So when a three-day teaching seminar held by CLASS (Christian Leaders, Authors, and Speakers Services) was offered near my home, I signed up. At that point, I had been addressing crowds for eight months with no formal training, and I was looking for an opportunity to refine my skills. Besides, the CLASS staff includes some prominent figures in the Christian industry — Florence Littauer, Marita Littauer, Georgia Shaffer — and it certainly couldn't hurt to rub elbows with them, right? One never knows where that might lead.

I can name the tune of those three days in one single word: humiliating.

As part of the training, each person had to do three different presentations on a subject they'd never spoken about before. The first two presentations were completely impromptu, and we were only given a few minutes to prepare for them. I am not a fan of impromptu anything — I'm the one who plans dinner menus months in advance — and I'm certainly not comfortable talking about an unfamiliar subject. Everyone else in the group was in the same boat, but we all survived the first two days and we learned a lot.

The third presentation was different. Each person was randomly assigned a Bible verse, and we had overnight to prepare a short presentation on it. I was excited. *I can do this. I have plenty of time to plan it, write it, and practice it. I'll even memorize it, so it'll flow smoother. And I'll use props! That'll really impress them.* So I went home on the evening of day two and wrote a brilliant composition on my assigned Bible verse, which was 1 Peter 3:15. "…Always be prepared to give an answer to everyone who asks you to give the reason for the hope that you have. But do this with gentleness and respect" (NIV).

This was the basic outline of my program:

> *If I were a defense attorney, I would need to prepare for my client's trial. As Christians, we are sometimes asked to defend our faith and explain the hope that is in us. We become defense attorneys for God, and therefore, we must present our CASE. We must Comprehend the Word of God. We must Apply it, Share it, and Exemplify it.*
>
> *Comprehend Scripture: Study it. Immerse ourselves in it. Allow God to speak to us through it.*
>
> *Apply it: To our own lives (so people can see that evidence of our hope), and to help others apply it to their lives.*
>
> *Share it: God gives us so many opportunities to spread His message of hope.*
>
> *Exemplify it: Always remember that we repre-*

sent God, so we must demonstrate His character and nature.

What is the evidence of our hope? A baby in a manger, a man on a cross, and an empty tomb. The defense rests. CASE closed.

Now for the props.

I used my creative talents to make four large cardboard placards spelling out C-A-S-E with the full word it stood for spelled out next to each letter. I intended to use plenty of examples from our everyday lives. I cut out pictures of a courtroom from a magazine as an illustration. I planned to describe a scene from the movie *Contact* (with Jodie Foster and Matthew McConaughey) and hold up the actual DVD for even more visual effect. I committed the entire presentation to memory and felt good about it. I was all ready to go. I was gonna nail this, for sure. Maybe they'll even ask me to speak for their national conference.

The next day, when it was my turn to present, I began to set up in front of the group. I was surprised to see that there was *no* podium for my notes. Since I only had two hands, four cardboard letters, two magazine cutouts, and a DVD case, something had to go. I decided my notes were not necessary. After all, I had the whole script memorized. *It'll be fine*, I told myself. I began the presentation.

I got to the *A* in CASE and I froze. *What does the A stand for? What's the next line? Oh, this is my worst nightmare come to life! I'm having a blackout. My notes! Oh no, they're not here! Think! Think! What's the A? Anticipate. No. Align. No. Advise. No. Approach. No. What is it?!*

I was panicking. But as dreadful as that was, I then committed the unthinkable act. The oratory *faux pas*. The cardinal sin of public speaking...

133

I asked if I could start over.

The group leader's firm answer was: "No. Just keep going." I skipped the A and moved on to the S. By that time, my mind was consumed with embarrassment, and I forgot all about the props. I struggled to finish the presentation, and when I finally did, I just wanted to disappear from the Earth and never be seen or heard from again. *I can flawlessly give my one-hour testimony to any size audience, but I can't even do a five-minute skit on 1 Peter 3:15. Florence Littauer is probably wondering what I'm even doing here, wasting her time.*

I call it The Tanya Harding Incident, referring to the 1994 Olympics where the champion figure skater started her routine, then fell, pathetically whimpered, and asked the judges if she could start over (after arranging an attempt to incapacitate teammate Nancy Kerrigan). Okay, at least I didn't plot to sabotage the other speakers. But I was discouraged and disgraced, and my confidence took a big hit. I went right home and talked to God about it.

What happened back there, Lord? You usually do all the talking — we're a team, remember? Why did you let me fall? Don't take this personally, but I no longer have a warm place in my heart for 1 Peter 3:15, and I'm never, ever using props again.

Perhaps God's strategy was to step back and let me do it all by myself so I would know what it feels like to fail. So I would once again realize my need for total dependency on Him. So I would experience what it's like to *really* be all alone up there.

Or maybe His plan was simply to expand my borders and once again take me out of my comfort zone. To see how I would handle a crisis. To equip me for the possibilities ahead. God took my training wheels off, gave me a little push, and I wiped out.

But learning how to ride a bike sometimes means falling off — it's all part of the growth process.

Or maybe God needed a way to reveal my two big faults: overconfidence and pride.

I had never before spoken without my notes in front of me. I've never needed them (until that day) and that made me overconfident. Couple that with the fact that I was using props for the first time — which created a distraction for me — and I got myself into trouble. I was relying completely on myself for the outcome and not on God. But God was merciful and compassionate by allowing me to crash in a classroom setting among my peers, instead of crashing at a ticketed event.

And then there's my pride. Once we become overconfident, our pride usually skyrockets. Once our pride skyrockets, it's all over. We become self-absorbed and consumed with our own success, and we take our eyes off of God. On that day, it was far too important for me to impress the leaders of the seminar and the other students in the group. It was all about me; it was all about what I could do. It *should have been* all about God and what He can do.

The apostle Paul wrote about this in his second letter to the Corinthians when he spoke of the thorn in his flesh. We don't know what affliction Paul had — and it really doesn't matter — but he said it was given "to keep me from exalting myself" (2 Corinthians 12:7, NASB). Thorns in our life have a purpose, but our reaction to the thorns is what determines the outcome of that purpose. We encounter thorns of disappointment, thorns of sickness, thorns of loss, thorns of failure. Depending on how we respond to the thorns, God will either use them for good... or Satan will use them for evil.

The Tanya Harding Incident — my thorn of failure — was traumatic enough... I sure didn't want Satan to claim a victory from it. So I asked God to use it to teach me something... and He did: I *will* use props in my programs again. (In fact, I do it quite often now.) I *will* always keep my notes handy. (I won't rely on my memory.)

And I *will* remember Who is truly the Star of the show.

·tf·

On the shores of the Sea of Galilee

Continuing Studies:
My Israel Prayer Journal

27

I can still re-member the day that Pastor Fisher announced to our church that he was organizing a trip to the Holy Land and that it was scheduled for March of 2005. As soon as he said the words, I knew instantly — without any hesitation — that I was going to Israel. And from that moment on, I counted the months... weeks... days until our departure.

Our church helps to support a Child Evangelism Fellowship missionary in Israel — Fadi Ramadan of Nazareth. When Fadi heard that I would be visiting Nazareth, he asked me to give my testimony at his church — a congregation of Arab Christians. As if my excitement about simply being in the Holy Land wasn't enough, the thought of actually speaking there was almost too much to contain. I knew this would be the trip of a lifetime... and I wasn't disappointed.

My family and friends thought I had lost my mind, traveling to the Middle East during a war. I tried to put their minds at ease before I left, because I had absolutely no fear about going there and I trusted God completely with my life. When my mother expressed her concern about the trip after hearing about a suicide bombing in Tel Aviv, I told her, "Mom, I'll be walking where Jesus walked and speaking where Jesus spoke. If I happen

to die where Jesus died, it doesn't get much better than that —
except for when I see Him!" That was clearly *not* any comfort to
her, since her mouth dropped, and she lost all color in her face
and ran out of the room.

I knew that this trip would make the Bible positively come
alive, since I would be able to recognize and envision so many
places in history as I read about them. I wanted to learn as much
as I could about the life and ministry of Jesus... so what better
way than to spend time in His footsteps?

Thanks to my nephew Kevin, I now write to God each day
— ever since he gave me a prayer journal for Christmas of 2001
and encouraged me to put down my thoughts and prayers in
writing. It has become a vital part of my daily routine, and it continued while I traveled throughout Israel. It was a joy for me to
write this Holy Land journal, it is a blessing to relive these
memories as I re-read it, and it is my honor to share them with
you now...

Sunday, March 6, 2005

Shalom my dear Lord Jesus,
I can't believe I'm here — in Tel Aviv. If anyone told me three
years ago that I would be this excited to go to Israel, I never
would have believed them. Back then I had absolutely no interest
in the biblical history of the Holy Land... and sadly, I had no interest in You, either. But that was my old self. My new self wants
so much to know You better, to get closer to You, to learn about
how and where You lived while You were here. And so I place
this trip into Your hands, Lord — please do with it whatever You
wish. I hope You will use it to teach our group and to expand
our knowledge and our relationship with You.

I thank You, Lord, for getting us here safely and for Your traveling mercies. The security at the airport was unlike anything I have ever experienced. I, for one, fully appreciated it. I couldn't help thinking that if other airlines had been that diligent with security in the past, Jim might still be here with me today.

Although, I'm certain that we never would have taken a trip to Israel.

Thank You, Lord, for everyone in our group. And thank You for giving us our Tour Guide Extraordinaire, David... we couldn't have asked for anyone better, and we feel blessed that he has been chosen to show us around his country.

Monday, March 7, 2005

Shalom my dearest Lord Jesus,
We stopped for lunch on the way back to our hotel, where we had lamb and liver kabobs (well, *I didn't* have liver), and I saw the first (of what I assume will be many) armed Israeli soldiers patrolling the area. I admit it's a bit unsettling to see eighteen-year-old boys *and girls* walking around with machine guns. I'm quite sure my mother would have gasped out loud and started praying at the sight of them. Lord, I ask You to please give her (and the rest of my family) peace about this trip. Help them to remember, as I do, that the outcome is always Yours.

By the way, Tel Aviv isn't anything to write home about, unless you're into pagan pleasure practices. It's one of the three major cities in Israel, and it has been said that: "Haifa works, Tel Aviv plays, and Jerusalem prays." From what I see, Lord, they really need You here in Tel Aviv — they just don't know it yet!

Tuesday, March 8, 2005

Shalom my dearest Lord Jesus,

Yesterday, we visited Jaffa (Joppa in the Bible) — the oldest operating seaport in the world (more than 3500 years old) from the time of the prophet, Jonah. You told Jonah to go east and bring Nineveh to repentance. Instead, he deliberately sailed off in completely the opposite direction, encountered a nasty storm, and ended up in the belly of a fish for three days... not a pleasant place to be. Fortunately for Jonah, there was a happy ending and he made his peace with You. I can think of many times in my life, Lord, when I disobeyed You — through deceit, idolatry, lack of restraint — and I had to deal with the consequences of my actions. Thank You for rescuing me from my own destructive behavior, even if it meant that I needed to be stuck in the belly of 9/11 to realize it.

Today we visited the ruins of the ancient town of Caesarea Maritima on the Mediterranean. King Herod built this port city in 22 B.C., and Pontius Pilate lived here during his terms as governor. Peter brought the Gospel here to the Roman centurion Cornelius, who became the first Gentile to convert to Christianity. It amazes me, Lord, how You work through plain, old, ordinary people like Peter to bring a corrupt city back to You. I pray that You will somehow use everyone in our group, through our adventure here in Israel, to assist in Your divine plans.

Tonight we arrived at our kibbutz on the Sea of Galilee. It is dark outside and I can't see much; but I do know that my room faces the water and, by the flickering lights, I can see that I have a spectacular view of the city of Tiberias across the sea. I have waited for this moment for a long time, and I don't want to wait any longer... I want to put my feet in the Sea of Galilee *right now.*

✦ ✦ ✦

Okay, Lord, I'm back. I walked down to the water with a few of the others in the group, took off my socks and shoes, rolled up my pants, and waded in just below my knees. The water was frigid — but then again, I'm the one who scuba dives with a full wetsuit in the 80-degree Caribbean, so my thermostat can't be trusted.

So there I was, standing in the Sea of Galilee in the dark, barely able to process the moment... Your presence here so long ago, the backdrop for so much of Your ministry, the significance of that water... how often You demonstrated Your sovereignty here, yet so many doubted and rejected You anyway.

Did You ever come here alone at night and let these gentle waves break on Your feet? Did You feel as refreshed and comforted as I do right now?

I stood in that cold water with only the light of the moon and a nearby lamp post, and I felt a sense of complete peace and serenity. When You were here, You knew You would soon bear the weight of the world on Your shoulders so that one day I could experience this peace. How can I even begin to thank You for this? I love You so much, Jesus.

Wednesday, March 9, 2005

Shalom my dearest Lord Jesus,
The alarm clock rang this morning, I opened my eyes, looked out the window, and saw the Sea of Galilee for the first time in daylight. Although it was raining and cloudy (I could barely see Tiberias), I still felt that same sense of awe and gratitude to You for bringing me here to this extraordinary place.

Today we went to Kursi, the site of the Miracle of the Swine (Luke 8:26–39). This is where You healed the demon-possessed man by sending the evil spirits into a large herd of pigs — the pigs promptly ran down a hill into the Sea of Galilee and drowned. That must have been a wild scene, Lord. It almost sounds like something from a Monty Python movie.

At each site we visit, a passage of Scripture is read to the group, describing the events that took place there. Then Pastor Fisher gives a short devotional, and we all sing a hymn. At Kursi, Mike read the passage about the swine from the Gospel of Luke. I sat outdoors with the rest of the group on the bottom step of the ruins of an ancient sixth-century Byzantine church altar and listened to Mike's words. My head was bowed, my eyes were closed, and the enormity of this whole thing hit me — *I am here right now, You were here two thousand years ago, and Your divine power is incomprehensible.* Tears began streaming down my face. I felt a gentle tapping on my right arm. I thought it was one of the other girls in the group — either giving me emotional support or maybe trying to get my attention — but instead I opened my eyes to find... a cat. It was tenderly stroking my arm with its little paw, then it began to rub up against my side. Now Lord, *You know* I am *not* a fan of cats. In fact, I downright despise them. So what was that all about? Did You actually send a *stray cat* to comfort me?

Everyone in the group thought this cat and its sensitivity to my emotional state was absolutely charming... and I admit, it was pretty cute. I couldn't help but think of Jim — he adored cats. For some reason, this cat would not leave me alone. There were thirteen other people it could have rubbed up against, but it chose me — the one person least likely to pet it. It continued to nuzzle its head into my side and tap its paw on my arm. *Are you trying to tell me something, Lord? Are You trying to teach me* to like cats? *Maybe this is a conspiracy — did Jim put You up to this?* The one animal that I typically avoid at all costs turned a tearful moment into a cheerful moment. A cat actually brought a smile to my face. (Congratulations, You just performed another miracle.) Maybe You're teaching me to broaden my horizons. Maybe you're teaching me to stop disregarding anything and everything that doesn't fit my definition of *normal*. Maybe You're teaching me to be willing to change.

We also visited the ruins of Bethsaida and Capernaum — two (out of three) ancient cities where You spent most of Your ministry. Capernaum is where You set up Your headquarters — I'm sure it was a nice piece of real estate in Your time. As I walked through the remains of these towns, it felt so surreal to know that You had walked here on these very same stone roads. You spent so much time here, teaching people… healing them… loving them. Yet they rejected You, refusing to repent and follow You. They refused to change. So You condemned all three cities. All were ultimately destroyed, never rebuilt, and still lay in ruins — just as You had predicted.

Whew, that could have been me. *Wait a minute — that was me, except I wasn't condemned.* Thank You, Jesus, for not giving up on me, even when I almost gave up on You… or when I refused — for so long — to repent of my old ways and start making major character improvements. I know I can be stubborn; I know I still resist change; I know I have a long way to go. But I am grateful that You care enough about me to reveal my weaknesses and help me to bring about those changes… I love You so much, Lord.

At our stop in Tabgha, where You fed five thousand people with two fish and five loaves of bread (Mark 6:30–44), I noticed a sign on a fenced-off area: "Private — No Entry." Carol and I asked David (our tour guide) what that was all about. He told us it was Dal Manutha, the quiet place on the water where You often came to be alone and pray. It is considered extremely sacred and holy and is usually not open to the public. Then he told us what *Dal Manutha* means in Hebrew... it means *widow*, as in *to be alone*.

We took a boat ride across the Sea of Galilee, and I saw Dal Manutha from the boat. There is a simple, wooden cross marking Your spot on the grassy shore of a small peninsula. Like a widow's solitude... it was Your solitude. I know it well.

✦ ✦ ✦

The sea was beautiful and calm today, though I've heard it is susceptible to sudden, violent storms. You know all about that, right? There You were, sailing across the Sea of Galilee with Your disciples — perhaps the very same course we took today — You were exhausted and asleep in the boat when they woke You up in a panic because a storm had blown in and the boat was sinking. (*"Teacher, don't You care that we're perishing?!?"*) These guys were seasoned fishermen; they must have been used to dealing with inclement maritime weather... so I suppose that must have been one wicked squall for them to call a state of emergency. I envision You climbing out of the stern still half asleep and nonchalantly commanding the wind to stop and the sea to calm down. (*"Peace, be still."*) And of course, it did.

Lord, I can think of so many times when I became annoyed — no, angry — with You because it appeared as though You were asleep on the job... particularly after 9/11. *Lord, are You there? Did You take the day off from work? Are You busy helping someone else? Why aren't You helping me? I'm sinking down here, and You don't seem to care one bit. Wake up and do something, will You?!?* I doubted Your power, I doubted Your ability to be in total control, and I'm sorry. I understand now that my life will not always be smooth sailing. But I trust you, my Captain, to navigate my life through rough waters.

Within a few hours, we went from sailing on the Sea of Galilee to climbing to the top of Mount Arbel. This was a bonus for us — not part of our tour schedule — but what a highlight! We saw the most magnificent view of the whole Galilee region... the entire sea, the surrounding towns, the majestic green mountains and landscapes... absolutely breathtaking! So I thank You, Lord, for giving us the opportunity to see the glory You have created in this land...

Tomorrow night I will be speaking to a group of Arab Christians at the church in Nazareth. Lord, You know the concerns I have about this program, and I lay my anxieties at Your feet. Speaking with a translator is a challenge, as I found out in Italy last summer. I pray that I don't become distracted and that the message doesn't get lost as Fadi (our missionary) translates my English into Arabic. Please give me and Fadi clarity of mind and speech, and give the people open minds and hearts. Lord, they often deal with persecution and threats of violence... please use this message to give them hope and encouragement.

Thursday, March 10, 2005

Shalom my dearest Lord Jesus,
Our first stop today was at the Mount of Beatitudes, where You preached the Sermon on the Mount (Matthew 5). It rained all morning, but we would never let that stop us from visiting any sites... we just took cover under the balcony of the church roof. Pastor Fisher asked *me* to read the Scripture passage for this

sight. His invitation blew me away — what an enormous privilege, Lord!

I told the group how significant this was for me. I told them about a conversation I once had with a Christian friend over twenty years ago... he mentioned "The Beatitudes," and I retorted, "The Beati*what?*" I had never heard of them before, nor did I care to hear about them back then. His constant references to You made me feel awkward and uncomfortable and I dismissed him promptly. Of course, I regret that now. Who would have thought — way back then — that I would one day be in Israel, standing on the spot where You stood, reading the Sermon on the Mount? A Beatitude is a declaration of blessing, and I declare that this was a tremendous blessing indeed.

Then You gave me even more evidence of Your power and presence. When we all turned our Bibles to Matthew chapter 5, the rain stopped and the sun came out! I took a slow, deep breath and began to read it out loud for the group... I got all choked up when I came to the verse that says, "Blessed are those who mourn, for they shall be comforted," and recognized the absolute truth in Your Word and the enormity of the moment. By Your grace I got through the rest of it without completely falling apart. The rain was gone, and the sun was brightly shining upon me the whole time I read the passage. The mist and clouds over the Sea of Galilee were right behind me. There were birds singing everywhere. But the greatest part is that I knew You were with us... You had been there before... You had said those words before...

148

> *Blessed are the poor in spirit, for theirs is the kingdom of heaven.*
> *Blessed are those who mourn, for they shall be comforted.*

Blessed are the gentle, for they shall inherit the earth.

Blessed are those who hunger and thirst for righteousness, for they shall be satisfied.

Blessed are the merciful, for they shall receive mercy.

Blessed are the pure in heart, for they shall see God.

Blessed are the peacemakers, for they shall be called sons of God.

Blessed are those who have been persecuted for the sake of righteousness, for theirs is the kingdom of heaven.

Blessed are you when people insult you and persecute you, and falsely say all kinds of evil against you because of Me.

Rejoice and be glad, for your reward in heaven is great...

— Matthew 5:3–12 (NASB)

Lord, this was one of the most deeply spiritual moments I have ever experienced, and I'm crying now just writing about it. Thank You, Jesus, for Your tender mercies... I am so grateful to You (and Pastor Fisher) for giving me this extraordinary experience. It is engraved upon my mind and I will remember it forever...

✦ ✦ ✦

After a few more stops, we finally came to Nazareth. This is where You grew up, Lord... yet when You returned here years later to preach, the people didn't recognize You as the Son of God... they recognized You as the son of Joseph and Mary and they rejected You. But You were back in the ol' neighborhood tonight... *with us.*

The town is quite a bit different than when You hung out here, wouldn't You say? The streets are crowded, noisy, and chaotic... it doesn't feel like part of the Holy Land. Years ago, Nazareth had a Christian majority. Now, the population is predominantly Muslim. Tonight I addressed a group of Arab Christians, who welcomed our group with open arms and warm hearts.

Fadi did an outstanding job translating my words into Arabic... what an exceptional gift You have given him! He not only converted the language so quickly and easily, but he expressed it with such passion and emotion. Many people asked us later if we had practiced it... we said, no, that it was the Spirit of Christ working it all out! As I looked into the faces in the audience, I knew it was hitting home for them. Their town and their country have been victims of hostility and persecution since the beginning of time. I believe my testimony simply confirmed what they already knew: The truth of Your promise, Jesus, when You said, "...In the world you will have trouble. But take heart! I have overcome the world" (John 16:33, NIV). What a tremendous comfort to all of us.

Thank you, Lord, for the opportunity to meet these extraordinary people. Thank You for having the confidence in me and Fadi to work for You. Thank You for everyone who attended the service and for the positive feedback they gave me. I thank You for the young man who stood up at the end and said, "I know it was meant for me to come tonight and hear this." I ask You to bless him, along with all the others, and keep them safe in Your tender care.

And I pray for their peace, Lord.

Friday, March 11, 2005

Shalom my dearest Lord Jesus,

Each morning before breakfast, I've been walking down to the sea by myself and just sitting... talking to You... enjoying the peace and quiet and beauty... and (ahem) collecting a few stones and shells to smuggle back home. I imagine what it must have been like when you called Peter and Andrew from the shores of this water and told them to follow You. I try to visualize You walking on the water in the storm. So many extraordinary, miraculous events happened here, and You continue to make extraordinary things happen in my life every day. More than anything, I praise You for Your sovereignty and glory... my Creator, my Savior, my Best Friend... I know that from this point forward for the rest of my life, every time I read about the Sea of Galilee in the Bible, it will take me right back to these mornings I have spent here with You.

Today we started out in Tel Dan, which is a nature reserve on the northern border of Israel. This place dates back to the nineteenth century B.C., and we know from the book of Genesis that Abraham was here. (Wow!) We saw many ancient ruins of walls and gates and a pagan altar built by King Jeroboam (circa 900 B.C.) to persuade the people away from worshipping You at the temple in Jerusalem. Times haven't changed too much, have they, Lord? We can turn on the TV, surf the Internet, walk through a shopping mall, or look at billboards to find plenty of pagan altars in our world today. They're just not built with ancient bricks and mud and stone.

Next was a stop at Banias, which in Your time was called Caesarea Philippi. It was yet another pagan ritual site for the Romans where the gods Pan and Zeus were worshipped. We saw the huge sacrificial altar and many large niches carved out of the mountainous rock. The niches were used as shrines to hold the statues of the god-of-this and the god-of-that. I know You visited here, Jesus, and I'm sure it must have greatly disturbed You to see those pagan temples and the spiritual ignorance of the people.

In fact, You had a very interesting little conversation with Your disciples here at Caesarea Philippi, which is recorded in Matthew 16:13–20. You asked them, "Who do people say that I am?" And they answered, "Some say You're Elijah, some say you're John the Baptist, others say You're a prophet..." Then You asked, "But who do *you* say that I am?" That's when Peter declared for the first time and without any reservation that You are the Messiah. A monumental moment right there in Caesarea Philippi.

Someone in our group suggested that I should be hoisted up into one of the ancient shrines in the wall of the mountain for an exclusive photo op. I looked at this carved-out hole in the rock (which was at least ten feet off the ground), shrugged my shoulders, and said, "Sure, if you can get me up there." So Chad cupped his hands, and I stepped one foot into them... Ed took my other leg and boosted me up... I grabbed onto the small opening of the shrine for all I was worth and pulled myself in with every ounce of strength I had. *I'm in! I'm in!* I positioned myself inside the cozy niche and laughed so hard (with everyone else) while cameras and camcorders shot the whole thing.

It wasn't the first time that Jennifer the Roman (Sicilian) Goddess had her own shrine, right Lord? One of my biggest character flaws is the belief that it's all about me; I lapse into that one a lot. It's my perpetual desire for control and power. It's my "I'm in charge here" attitude. It's my Evita-esque nature. I know I exhibited that commanding behavior many times with Jim and for thirty-eight years of my life with You. And as I sat inside my made-to-order shrine in Caesarea Philippi, the humbling truth of it once again hit me. *Whoa, what am I doing up here? Yeah, it's a harmless antic, but it's a bit too close to reality. It's not about me, Lord. It's all about You. Okay, I've had enough! I'd like to come down now!*

Getting down from the shrine was a bit more challenging than being hoisted up. This time it took three guys to do it, and I basically had to take a deep breath and fall — feet first — with the hope that they'd catch me. Thank You, Lord, for gently reminding me of my unauthorized and undeserved dominion... at the very same place where Peter confidently stated Your rightful and divine dominion.

Saturday, March 12, 2005

Shalom my dearest Lord Jesus,
We left the Galilee region this morning... we're heading south toward the Dead Sea, and we'll be making some stops along the way. I miss Galilee already, especially the sea. It was so quiet and peaceful there, and I know it will be a much different atmosphere once we reach Jerusalem.

Our first stop was in Yardenit, which is the baptismal site on the Jordan River. By the way, Lord, that "mighty Jordan" isn't so mighty. Maybe it was back in Your time, but now it's more like the Jordan brook. Or the Jordan creek. Or the Jordan stream. Nevertheless, it's where You and John baptized believers, and Yardenit is the specific area where it's done today.

You know I couldn't leave there without putting my feet in the Jordan River. I considered being baptized (*re*-baptized) there, but I quickly decided against it after I took that first step into the freezing cold water. Being immersed in it — then traveling in cold, wet clothes all day — would not have been a wise move.

153

But I stood ankle-deep in the water and prayed that You would accept my weak gesture as a symbol of my re-commitment to You. Just because I haven't submerged my body underwater doesn't mean I haven't submerged my heart in You…

We took the long drive south to the Dead Sea. In order to get there, we had to drive through the West Bank. It isn't often that a bus full of fourteen excited tourists becomes completely silent for any length of time, but that was indeed the case today, as David explained the harsh reality of the current political situation: "Several well-supported, well-funded, and well-armed Palestinian guerrilla organizations are at war with Israel. Their presence in the West Bank can make it dangerous to travel here. The territory we are driving through is considered 'Area A' — it is under PLO control, and it is critical that all vehicles stay on the main road and pass through security checkpoints. Departing from the designated roadway puts Israeli vehicles at risk for stoning and/or shooting." Needless to say, we stayed on the main road.

The history of this major conflict is long and complicated — but the bottom line is that many Palestinian groups refuse to negotiate with Israel, and many Israelis cannot bear the idea of relinquishing any part of the Promised Land. Throughout our solemn journey through the West Bank, David pointed out evidence of this ongoing hostility: an enormous electric fence put up by the Palestinians runs along the border of Jordan. Barbed-wire fences surround and protect the few Jewish settlements that remain. Field after field of countless small, yellow signs warn of unexploded land mines, and of course, we saw more teenage soldiers carrying machine guns.

154   The reality of this divided, disputed region is depressing to look at, Lord — yet how much more agonizing it must be for those who are directly involved in it. The Arabs and the Jews who live here are constantly dealing with harsh conditions; they

will likely never know peace... but for us, we simply put those images aside almost as soon as we left the West Bank. *We apologize for the sobering interruption. Back to our regularly scheduled program.*

And just like that, my mind switched gears as we stopped for a bathroom break after leaving the West Bank. There, in the parking lot of a rest stop, I rode a camel (a Bedouin Arab was offering rides, I couldn't resist) and I quickly forgot about the political chaos we had just driven through.

Finally we arrived at the Dead Sea, which is the lowest place on earth (1300 feet below sea level) and contains the saltiest water on earth (almost 40 percent salinity, hence the reason why they call it the *Dead* Sea since nothing can live in it). The Sea is exceptionally beautiful with the rocky desert mountains surrounding the azure water... then it gets weird. There are giant salt pillars that look like mushroom-shaped icebergs protruding from the water, and people float in the water like bobbing corks. Lord, You are amazing. Your creations blow my mind. I wonder what You were thinking when You designed this one.

Our hotel is a luxury spa resort located right on the shore. Unfortunately, we're only here for one night — but I am grateful to You, Lord, for this special treat and for the magnificent view of the sea from my room!

The first thing Rosemary and I did was to explore the spa and see what kind of new adventure we could get ourselves into. We got ourselves into a mud bath — an unforgettable first for me. We each had our own private room where Ada — who didn't speak English — plastered us with thick, hot, black mud from neck to toe, then wrapped us tightly in clear plastic (like a mummy). I laid like that on a comfortable table for thirty minutes, unable to move and drenched in a marinade of mud that looked and felt (but definitely did not taste) like hot fudge. Ada occasionally came into the room to place a cold cloth on my forehead and let me sip water through a straw, so I wouldn't dehydrate.

For the first ten minutes, I could not stop laughing. Ada must have thought I was an American fool. It started as a chuckle but quickly worked itself into uncontrollable hilarity. All I could think of was Jim and what his reaction would be to see his crazy wife dipped in Willy Wonka dark chocolate sauce. I imagined how ridiculous I must have looked — I imagined Jim shaking his head and rolling his eyes and saying, "Oh brother. I knew it would come to this. She's finally lost her mind." Then I realized that my irrepressible laughter was counterproductive to the purpose of relaxation, so I tried to get control of myself. *Please God, grant me the serenity to get a grip here.*

But then I started thinking about You, Lord, and what You would make of all this... and I started laughing all over again, because I envisioned *You* — shaking *Your* head and rolling *Your* eyes and saying, "That's not really what I intended when I created mud, but if it makes you happy, go for it."

After I finally broke the laughter marathon, I used the rest of the time to pray. Ada eventually came back into the room and helped me slither into the shower to rinse the mud off — took me a while and made a big mess — then our instructions were to immediately bathe in the Dead Sea for the finishing touch. (The high mineral content of the hot mud followed by the cool, salty seawater is supposed to be therapeutic for the skin and for rheumatic conditions. Sounds like a good prescription to me.)

As I floated in the sea like a buoy, I reflected on what You might say about my little spa adventure. The mud is like our sins. It might feel really good while you're doing it, but the fact of the matter is that it's still mud. It's dark and dirty, and it corrupts and disguises any goodness in our character underneath.

You are the shower, Jesus. With Your cleansing blood, You wash away our sins. The sea is our ongoing relationship with You... but I call you the Living Sea, not the Dead Sea, because You are the living water and the salt. You preserve us, heal us, nourish us, flavor us. You keep us afloat — You do not let us sink. You continue to cleanse us when the mud surfaces, or when we disobey You and take another dip in it. Thank You, Lord, for our safety while traveling today... and for camel rides and mud baths and salt swims.

Sunday, March 13, 2005

Shalom my dearest Lord Jesus,
After stuffing myself with five bowls of porridge at breakfast this morning, we left our hotel on the Dead Sea and headed for Masada. It was a beautiful, warm, perfect, sunny day — thank You, Lord!

Masada is located at the top of an isolated mountain next to the Dead Sea. The mountain has a flat peak on which Herod built a three-tiered palace fortress (circa 36 B.C.). After he died and after the Temple Mount in Jerusalem was destroyed in 70 A.D., Masada became a refuge for Jewish zealots. When the Romans came to conquer the fortress, the 967 Jewish zealots realized they had no chance for freedom; so they decided to take their own lives rather than become slaves of the Romans. Ten men were chosen (by a lottery system) to kill everyone else — then the ten killed each other, and the last man killed himself. Only two women and five children survived to tell the story — they had chosen a life of slavery instead of death. I honestly have to wonder, Lord, what my decision would have been given their same set of circumstances. *To live is Christ and to die is gain...*

The story is sad but the excavations are so impressive. There were some loose mosaic tiles and broken pieces of ancient pottery on the ground, a few of which found their way into my pocket. (The rule is: it's okay to take loose rocks and artifacts from the ground as long as you don't dig them out.) I found a really nice chunk of broken pottery, which looked like it could have been part of an ancient jug handle. Then I examined it more closely and realized it was a petrified piece of chewing gum. No need to spell out that lesson, Lord. I read you loud and clear.

The next stop was Ein Gedi, where soon-to-be King David and his men hid from King-for-the-time-being Saul (circa 1000 B.C.), and I can see why David chose Ein Gedi, Lord! I stand in awe of Your glory and majesty! The huge waterfalls... the lush greenery... the huge rock formations... the spectacular view of the Dead Sea... I could have stayed there all day. I wonder if David and his army hated to leave as much as I did.

After a few more stops, we were headed for Jerusalem. Our tour guide David has been such an exceptional blessing to us, Lord, and we thank You so much for his wisdom and knowledge, his patience and sense of humor. I remember how concerned I was before we arrived in Israel that our tour guide might not speak English well enough for us to understand his explanations. Of course, You already had that all worked out; it was never an issue. David speaks with a slight British accent, which we all find charming. This is Pastor Fisher's twenty-ninth trip to Israel... he said that of all the tour guides he's ever had, David is by far the best. Since we have a small group (only fourteen people), David has made a point of getting to know each one of us. David is Jewish — though he doesn't practice it — in fact, he is exceptionally well versed in the New Testament. He is a veteran of the Israeli army and served in Sinai in 1952. He has witnessed so many changes in this country, Lord, and he must surely wonder what lies ahead for the Israeli people. Our awesome bus driver, Benny, is a Russian Jew... a quiet, gentle man with kind eyes and a big heart. Lord, I ask You to please bless David and Benny for their desire and willingness to make our trip so memorable... and please keep them and their families safe in these unstable times.

We soon saw the three distinctive towers that pop out of the skyline of Jerusalem: Hebrew University, Augusta Victoria Hospital, and the Church of the Ascension. We knew we were getting close.

Just outside the city a new tunnel has been constructed to help with the traffic problem. And as the bus drove into the dark tunnel, David began singing *Jerusalem of Gold*, and the entire bus became silent (for the second time this week) as we listened to his words. His voice was powerful and passionate and spirited, and the song came from deep down in his loyal Israeli heart. It conveyed many bittersweet years of heartache and joy, and it was clear that Jerusalem was different for him than any other place we had visited...

> *The olive tree that stands in silence upon the hills of time,*
> *To hear the voices of the city as bells of evening chime.*
> *The Shofar sounding from the temple to call the world to prayer*
> *The Shepherd pauses in the valley and peace is everywhere*
> *Jerusalem, Jerusalem, Forever young, forever old.*
> *My heart will sing your songs of glory, Jerusalem!*

Jerusalem, Jerusalem, Oh, city with a heart of gold.
My heart will sing your songs of glory. Jerusalem!

Somehow David orchestrated the timing so that he sang while we were driving through the dark tunnel... then as soon as we emerged into the light with the magnificent city sprawled out in front of us, David finished his moving song and we applauded him.

And from the depths of his heart, he announced, "Ladies and Gentlemen, welcome to Jerusalem..."

I guess it was the way he said it. It sent chills down my spine, left a big lump in my throat, and shot a thousand emotions through my heart. So much significance in this place. So much has happened here, so much will happen here. I'm not going to pretend that I understand all the political and religious conflicts. I'm trying, Lord, but it gets so complicated. All I can do is what David asked us to do: pray. So I pray for the wisdom of the leaders in this country, Lord. I pray that they will turn to You for the answers and that You will open their hearts and their minds to Your truth, so they can make the right decisions. I pray that Your will — not theirs — be done.

Benny took us for a quick drive within the walls of the city before we checked into our hotel. We drove past the Mount of Olives; we saw all the ancient gates into the city; we saw the Dome of the Rock (the enormous gold-domed mosque) on top of the Temple Mount. As we drove, David reviewed Jerusalem's long religious and political history from ancient times until now: Within the ancient walls of the city is a collision of Jews, Christians, and Muslims — all with entirely different belief systems, different cultures, and different political opinions — yet they somehow co-exist. They all practice their faith within the confines of the walls, yet they all live remarkably separate and antagonistic lives. Jerusalem means: "City of Peace." Seems to me it's more like an expression of wishful thinking than reality, Lord.

Our hotel is wonderful, Lord, and I thank You for providing me with yet another lovely room and a beautiful view of the city from my window. After dinner I went for a walk with Mike, Donna, and Bill down to the Damascus gate. I still can't believe I'm here, Lord.

Monday, March 14, 2005

Shalom my dearest Lord Jesus,
At 4:30 A.M., I was startled awake by the sound of the Islamic prayer call coming from the minaret (tower) of a mosque, which is right outside my hotel window. The man's voice chanting the Arabic song broadcasted over loudspeakers, so that all Muslims in this neighborhood would hear it and be reminded to come to prayer. These resounding prayer calls can be heard five times throughout the day from all mosques. I just didn't expect one at 4:30 A.M.

Our first stop in Jerusalem was the Mount of Olives. We stood at an observation point on the top of the steep hillside and looked across the Kidron Valley at the entire city of Jerusalem — what a spectacular view, Lord! I was surprised to see that the Mount of Olives is not covered with olives. It's covered with thousands of white tombs — the largest and oldest continually used cemetery in the world. Graves dating back four thousand years rest beside modern ones; each tomb contains the bones of several generations of a single family. I never thought I could ever look at a cemetery and actually be... inspired.

We made our way down a steep path — the one that You probably took — down to the Dominus Flevit Church. The church is shaped like a teardrop, because it commemorates the place where You wept over Jerusalem during Your triumphal entry into the city... your last week here on Earth. Remember when You said, "'If you... had only known on this day what would bring you peace — but now it is hidden from your eyes. The days will come upon you when your enemies... will not leave one stone on another, because you did not recognize the time of God's coming to you'" (Luke 19:42–44, NIV)?

You cried for their close-mindedness. You grieved over the hardness of their hearts. You hurt for them, knowing the destruction that was yet to come. You surely must look at our lives and our mistakes — knowing the consequences of our actions — and feel that same hurt when we turn away from You. You can identify with every parent who helplessly watches their rebellious child choose the wrong fork in the road of their life. You stood on the ground where we stood today, and You knew the big picture. You knew what was ahead, and You wept.

From the moment I booked this trip, Lord, there was one spot that I looked forward to visiting more than any other: the Garden of Gethsemane. I remember from our trip to Italy that *Gethsemane* means *oil press* in Hebrew — it's a place where oil is squeezed from olives. In the Garden of Gethsemane, You were being squeezed. You came here with Your disciples after the last Passover meal... You prayed in agony to Your Father, knowing the pain and torture that You would very soon endure. Matthew's gospel says that You asked God three times to intervene: "'My Father, if it is possible, let this cup pass from Me; yet not as I will, but as You will'" (Matthew 26:39, NASB). But the cup of suffering was not taken from You; and right here in Gethsemane — Your favorite spot — You were betrayed and arrested.

162

The next day, the penalty of every sin of the entire human race — and the wrath of Your Father — was turned loose on You. The Garden of Gethsemane does not look like it did back in the days when You came here to pray. There was no church marking the spot. The olive trees were here back then, but there were no sidewalks creating paths between them. There was no busy highway running directly in front of this sacred spot. Nevertheless, it isn't difficult to imagine You being here. It just *feels* like You were here...

We all sat outside on some benches near the church and prayed, read from Scripture, sang a hymn... and tried to ignore the sound of speeding cars and honking horns on the busy road in front of us. We watched as Israeli soldiers arrested an Arab man and took him into custody, while his wife and young child nervously looked on. I have no idea what had transpired, but I wondered if someone had betrayed *him*. I wondered if he (or his wife) was praying... *if it is possible, let this cup pass from me; yet not as I will, but as You will.*

I know I've prayed it a few times myself, Lord. I may not have used Your exact words, but many times I have prayed for You to take my cup away. Sometimes I don't think I'm strong enough to drink from it. Sometimes I forget that You already have. Sometimes I think that there's poison in my cup, and I wonder why You would allow my lips to touch it. I forget that what appears to be poison might actually be a blessing in disguise.

I remember praying to You after 9/11 when I accepted You into my heart. In the Gethsemane of my living room, I waved the white flag of surrender and told You how sorry I was for the countless times I had hurt You and disappointed You. I made a commitment to trust You with my own cup of suffering. I remember sobbing and praying in agony (like You did) and saying these words:

163

Lord, I cannot believe what has happened to my life. I wish things were different... I wish Jim was still here. I don't understand it and I definitely don't like it. But I know I must accept it, and I know I must accept You as my only hope. So if You've got a plan to make something good out of this, then please go ahead with it. I'm all Yours.

Lord, I will never forget the brief time we spent in Gethsemane, and I thank You for bringing us there to see one of Your favorite places. I know that from now on, whenever I face a trial, I will imagine myself in the garden... surrounded by olive trees, remembering Your agony, and thanking You for bearing the cup and taking the cross for me.

St. Anne's Church is an acoustic paradise, Lord. We sat inside and listened while another tour group sang a hymn, and it was electrifying. There is an eight to ten second echo in that building, and I don't think it's possible for anyone to be off key — all the voices just kind of blend together in harmony, and it is absolutely spine tingling. When it was our turn, we sang *It Is Well with My Soul*, and the powerful sound of our voices resonated off the walls and ricocheted right back into my heart. That is Maria's favorite hymn and one of mine also... I wished so much that she and Tom could be here to experience this. Ah, but You provided a way for us to capture the moment and share it with our families back home: Mike recorded it, so we will always have this memory. Thank You, Lord. May it be a sweet, sweet sound to Your ears...

We left St. Anne's and made our way into the place where the Antonio Fortress once stood in Your time. The Bible calls this area the Praetorium (Place of Judgment); it is where You were tried and sentenced and Your physical suffering began. Today, the

Sisters of Zion Convent stands here, and there are two chapels that mark this solemn spot: The Church of the Flagellation and the Chapel of the Condemnation. The convent and the chapels contain the remains of the original scourging floor — large paved stones upon which You were flogged and beaten by Roman soldiers and crowned with thorns.

In the Chapel of Condemnation, Pastor Fisher once again asked *me* to do the Scripture reading. Me? Do *this* reading? Lord, I was a bit emotional over the Beatitudes — but now we're talking about *Your* trial and *Your* suffering. This is another whole level of emotion. And I was standing on the very floor where it all happened.

I opened my Bible to John 18 and started to read from verse 33:

> *Therefore Pilate entered again into the Praetorium, and summoned Jesus and said to Him, "Are You the King of the Jews?"*
>
> *Jesus answered, "Are you saying this on your own initiative, or did others tell you about Me?"*
>
> *Pilate answered, "I am not a Jew, am I? Your own nation and the chief priests delivered You to me; what have You done?"*
>
> *Jesus answered, "My kingdom is not of this world. If My kingdom were of this world, then My servants would be fighting so that I would not be handed over to the Jews; but as it is, My kingdom is not of this realm."*
>
> *Therefore Pilate said to Him, "So You are a king?"*
>
> *Jesus answered, "You say correctly that I am a king For this I have been born, and for this I have*

165

come into the world, to testify to the truth. Every-
one who is of the truth hears My voice."

Pilate said to Him, "What is truth?" And
when he had said this, he went out again to the
Jews and said to them, "I find no guilt in Him.
But you have a custom that I release someone for
you at the Passover; do you wish then that I re-
lease for you the King of the Jews?"

So they cried out again, saying, "Not this Man,
but Barabbas." Now Barabbas was a robber.

Pilate then took Jesus and scourged Him. And
the soldiers twisted together a crown of thorns and
put it on His head, and put a purple robe on
Him; and they began to come up to Him and say,
"Hail, King of the Jews!" and to give Him slaps in
the face.

Pilate came out again and said to them, "Be-
hold, I am bringing Him out to you so that you
may know that I find no guilt in Him." Jesus then
came out, wearing the crown of thorns and the
purple robe. Pilate said to them, "Behold, the Man!"

So when the chief priests and the officers saw
Him, they cried out saying, "Crucify, crucify!"

Pilate said to them, "Take Him yourselves and
crucify Him, for I find no guilt in Him."

The Jews answered him, "We have a law, and
by that law He ought to die because He made
Himself out to be the Son of God."

166

My heart was so heavy as I read those words... and I'm sure
everyone in our group felt the same sorrow for You, Lord. The
only thing that kept me from breaking down while I read the

passage was the noisy chatter of people standing in the doorway of the church. It was distracting and frustrating. I wanted to scream, "Be quiet! We are reading about our Lord's suffering, don't you care?" I had flashbacks of the many distractions I've dealt with when I spoke at bookstores. I wondered if You used those speaking engagements to help me prepare for this one. Well, I haven't mastered anything yet. It's still very hard for me to tune things out, Lord, especially when I'm doing something I consider vitally important. I stood on the scourging floor humbly reading from Your Word... battling my emotions... battling the distractions... and wondering why You would ever do what You did *for us.* We certainly didn't deserve it, and many of us don't even appreciate it... like the people standing in the doorway. Nevertheless, I am so grateful to Pastor Fisher for giving me yet another opportunity to read from Your Word — it is such a privilege, an honor, a gift. And attempting to express my gratitude to You for the suffering You endured for me is futile. I will never be able to thank You enough... but I'll never stop trying.

As we stepped out of the Chapel of the Condemnation, we stepped onto the Via Dolorosa. It is the road You took when You carried the cross to Calvary, where You were crucified.

David gave us a brief account of what happened to You on the Via Dolorosa — one we're all familiar with. Before we started the walk, he warned us that this street is full of expert pickpockets and that we must watch our pockets and purses, stay close to each other, and be aware of our surroundings. Even now, two thousand years later, this street still victimizes innocent people.

It was dirty. Seedy. Unsettling. It was lined with street peddlers who aggressively hustled us to buy their stuff. They obnoxiously yelled out as we passed them, "One dollah, one dollah! We have bracelet, we have postcard, we have olive wood, you come and have drink, one dollah, one dollah!"

I had anticipated an emotionally powerful, solemn walk down the Via Dolorosa. I thought the path would be held sacred and holy… but it was far from my expectations. I was continually sidetracked from the thoughts of what really happened to You there. I wanted to feel and experience Your suffering — if only in my mind. But the more I tried to envision the painful path You took for us, the more I became frustrated with the den of thieves and their lack of respect for You. I'm sure you experienced a lot of disrespect from the crowds who mocked You as You carried the cross. So what were You trying to teach me?

Satan will try everything in his power to divert our attention away from You. He tempts us with material things that distract us from the true meaning of Your sacrifice. He uses interruptions to redirect our vision away from the cross. Lord, please give me the focus to keep my eyes on You. Please give me the strength to tune out anything that might come between us. Please help me to control my disdain for the peddlers and pray as You did: *Forgive them, Father, for they know not what they're doing.*

But there's more. When it comes to showing appreciation for You and Your gift of eternal life, I have been just as guilty as the peddlers. Too many times in my life I have been apathetic, ignorant, and inconsiderate of Your sacrifice; and far too often I have failed and hurt and disappointed You. But it was for those sins that You did what You did for us. So please forgive *me*, Lord, for all the times when I chose to look away from You, *even when I knew exactly what I was doing.*

168 Tuesday, March 15, 2005

Shalom my dearest Lord Jesus,
I woke up at 4:30 A.M. again to the sound of the Islamic prayer

call. I used the opportunity to pray to You until I fell back to sleep. We would have liked to visit Bethlehem, but the area wasn't safe so David did not feel comfortable taking us there. There was a quiet spot where we were able to see it from a distance, and the Herodion (another one of Herod's mountaintop palaces that he named after himself) was in the background. Pastor Fisher made an interesting comment about the difference between the two kings who lived back then. Herod was the king of the world. He had more power, authority, and influence than any human on earth, and he wasn't afraid of anything or anyone... except that little Baby — the true King of Kings — who was born just a few miles away in Bethlehem. Herod was cruel, cunning, paranoid, and fearless — he killed everyone (including his favorite wife and two of his sons) who threatened his reign, and he tried unsuccessfully to kill You, Lord, when he heard about Your birth. It's two thousand years later, and Herod's glory, wealth, and grandeur are gone... all that's left are ruins. Whose kingdom still survives and always will? That little Baby born in Bethlehem. How cool is that, Lord...

Today we also spent time in the Valley of Elah — this is where David and Goliath had their big showdown (1 Samuel 17). We stopped at the brook from which David took five stones, put them in his slingshot, slung the first stone, clocked Goliath in the forehead, and killed him. It made me think about how You give each of us our own stones, slings, and skills necessary to fight our own battles — physical, emotional, spiritual, or otherwise. You give us special gifts and abilities and all the resources we need to get through every trial in our lives. Thank You, Lord, for giving me all the ammunition I needed to defeat my 9/11 Goliath of grief and depression.

Tonight after dinner, we all gathered together in Pastor Fisher's room to talk about our Israel experience (it's almost over... I can't believe it… don't want to go home, Lord.) Pastor went around the room, and we each took a turn sharing our two fondest memories of the trip. When it was my turn, I fumbled a bit… it wasn't easy to narrow it to two… but this is what I came up with:

Number one, reading the Sermon on the Mount on the Mount of Beatitudes. Number two, when David was singing as we drove into Jerusalem, and his words… *"Ladies and Gentlemen, welcome to Jerusalem."* Those are two powerful memories that inevitably stir up my emotions… although there are a hundred other memories that easily compete for first and second place.

Lord, in less than seventy-two hours we'll be on a plane back to New Jersey. I don't want to leave here, and I'm already praying for an opportunity to come back one day. I love You, Jesus. I thank You. I praise You. I worship You. I love You.

Wednesday, March 16, 2005

Shalom my dearest Lord Jesus,
Heard the loud chanting at 4:30 A.M. again, Lord. That's one thing I won't miss when we leave Israel.

We were in Jerusalem all day today, starting out at the Temple Mount (or Mount Moriah) where Jews, Christians, and Muslims place tremendous historical significance as a most holy site. On the Temple Mount stands The Dome of the Rock — the landmark of Jerusalem — and the third most important holy site (after Mecca and Medina) for the Muslims. Even though Muhammad never visited Jerusalem, Muslims believe that the rock is where he left the earth on his "Night Journey." The rock is the site where Abraham offered his son Isaac as a sacrifice to God. King Solomon built the first Temple there (circa 1000 B.C.) on the site of the rock, and it contained the Holy of Holies and the Ark of the Covenant (which housed the Ten Commandments). Jesus, You came here on several occasions from the time You were an infant up to the last week of Your life here on Earth. After the first Temple was destroyed, it was rebuilt and destroyed again and rebuilt and destroyed again… until finally, in the seventh century A.D., the Muslims acquired it and built the massive blue-tiled mosque with an enormous, gleaming dome of gold above the huge limestone rock.

Needless to say, this place is extremely sacred to all three religions. But the Temple Mount is prohibited to orthodox Jews, and it is only accessible to Christians if they obey very strict regulations. We had to go through two exhaustive security checks in order to enter. We were permitted to walk around the courtyard, but we were not allowed to enter the mosque itself, the Dome of the Rock. We came to a quiet and secluded area, and David, our tour guide, suggested that we pray together, which we did. A guard began yelling at us in Arabic, so we stopped praying and moved on. We asked David to translate what the guard had said. He replied, "The guard said, 'Don't ever do that again!' and I said in Arabic, 'Okay, we won't.' Then I muttered in English, 'Until next time.'" Then David shrugged his shoulders, grinned, and said to us, "I've been rebuked by better."

Lord, that experience made me so grateful to live in a country where we are free to pray to You and to choose and practice our beliefs without religious persecution. Thank You for reminding me of something we so often take for granted. I now have a much greater appreciation of that vital privilege, and I pray we will always have that freedom.

Our next stop was at St. Peter in Gallicantu, a church that commemorates the place where Peter denied You three times after You were arrested. It was built on top of the ruins of the house of Caiaphas, the high priest who passed You onto Pilate for judgment. Among the ruins were a prison cell and torture chambers. After You were arrested at Gethsemane, it's very possible that You were held in the prison cell of Caiaphas's house until You were tried by Pilate on Friday morning. Whatever the case, You were held in a cell somewhere... in some small, cold, damp, dark stone chamber... alone and abandoned by Your friends.

Our group stood inside the prison cell in Caiaphas's house. There was a large hole in the high ceiling where they would have dropped the prisoner (You?) down onto the cold, stone floor. I leaned against the ancient wall of the cell and felt its dampness. I looked around and imagined the horror of being here all by myself in complete darkness, like it was for You. Pastor Fisher did a reading (Psalm 88) which You might have recited by tradition as You waited to face Pilate in the morning. I recalled the sadness I felt for the apostle Paul when I stood in his prison cell in Rome. But this is different. This is about *You*, and You did this for *us*.

How alone You must have felt. You knew it would come to this. You prayed in agony about it just hours before in Gethsemane, asking Your Father to remove Your cup. Surely You continued to pray to Him all night long... and He must have seemed so silent and distant. He must have seemed as cold as the floor You were sitting on.

I have never spent the night in a prison cell. But I did spend many nights after 9/11 in the prison of a bedroom with an empty spot on the mattress next to me. My dear family and friends never abandoned me — many times they were just down the hall if I needed them — yet I had never felt so alone. I thought You had abandoned me, Lord. I thought You had turned Your back on my pain. I couldn't have been more wrong...

You were right there with me the whole time. That spot on the mattress wasn't empty — I just couldn't see You sitting there. You were patiently waiting for me to calm down and stop panicking. You were waiting for me to open my eyes and my heart and feel Your loving embrace. You know all about being alone in cold, dark prisons. You were sent here to live and to die for our sins... and to identify with us, so that we can identify with You. There is no trial that I have ever gone through — nor will ever go through — that You haven't already been through.

I cried in that prison cell today out of inexpressible gratitude and love for You and Your sacrifice for us. I cried because, even though You were left and forsaken, You will never leave us nor forsake us. I cried because I just don't know how to say thank You, Jesus.

✦ ✦ ✦

We also visited the Wailing Wall today. This is the holiest place of prayer for Jews, because it is the last remnant of the only sacred place in the world, the Temple Mount. Jews gather here to mourn the loss of their Temple and the Ark of the Covenant and to pray for the coming of the Messiah. They traditionally write prayers on scraps of paper, then they squeeze the paper into the gaps in the wall as they recite from the Torah. There are two sections — one for men, one for women — which follows the Orthodox practice.

I went with the ladies in our group into the women's section and found many Jewish women standing up against the wall as they prayed. A few of them were sobbing. I took a piece of scrap paper and scribbled a small prayer on it: "Dear Jesus, thank You for bringing us to Your Promised Land. Please help us to show people who You are, and please bring peace here. We love You." I took my place at the wall, among many Jewish women, and pressed my crumpled paper into a crack between two huge stones.

Although it was obvious that we were Christians unfamiliar

173

with their traditions, no one rebuked us for praying at their most sacred place. No one said, "Don't ever do that again!" No one reprimanded us when we didn't have a scarf covering our heads and shoulders — they just kindly handed one to us. I wondered what the Jewish women (and men) were praying about... no doubt for their lives, for their families, for their country, for their safety, for their Messiah to come. Not unlike my own prayers, I suppose, except I was praying for our Messiah to come *back*. It felt good to be here, Lord... I wanted to stay longer. I wanted to pray with them more.

But then You brought us to one of the highlights of our trip: Hezekiah's Tunnel. This is an underground water shaft built within the walls of the Old City by King Hezekiah around 800 B.C. — it runs over six hundred yards long and connects the Gihon Spring to the Pool of Siloam (where You healed the blind man). There is still water in the tunnel (knee-deep for most, thigh-deep for me), so we wore old clothes and shoes we didn't care about. It was pitch black down there, so we carried small flashlights and made our way through the winding tunnel.

Lord, I think this was the coolest thing I've ever done in my life! The passage was so narrow, and I constantly brushed up against the 2800-year-old stone walls. The bottom was made up of large, uneven rocks — and since it was dark, I had to feel my way with each step to keep my balance. Our voices echoed as we waded through, single file, and shined our lights on the person in front of us. A few times we stopped, turned off all our flashlights, and stood completely still in the water. And inside the 2800-year-old underground aqueduct... in total darkness... we sang a hymn.

As the deer panteth for the water, so my soul longeth after Thee

> *You alone are my heart's desire, and I long to
> worship Thee*
> *You alone are my strength, my shield; to You
> alone may my spirit yield*
> *You alone are my heart's desire, and I long to
> worship Thee*

We sounded so good, we decided to sing another one for You…

> *My hope is built on nothing less than Jesus' blood
> and righteousness*
> *I dare not trust the sweetest frame but wholly
> trust in Jesus' Name*
> *On Christ the solid Rock I stand*
> *All other ground is sinking sand*
> *All other ground is sinking sand*

The acoustics made our voices sound so incredibly awesome…
and standing in complete blackness was not frightening at all,
because the words of the hymns were comforting. In fact, the
darkness forced us to isolate ourselves with You, Lord. Singing
underground in the dark in knee-deep water was an indescrib-
ably welcome sensation. There were no other distractions — no
noisy traffic, no harassing street peddlers, no thunderous prayer
calls. Just You and us and 2800 years worth of history. Thank
You, Jesus, for this amazing experience. When I return home to
the reality of New Jersey — the emails, the phones ringing, the
meetings and appointments, the busy days at the pharmacy —
please help me to remember those moments in Hezekiah's Tunnel, so that I may once again feel that quiet peace and comfort
within the walls of Your love, Lord.

Thursday, March 17, 2005

Shalom my dearest Lord Jesus,

The Islamic prayer call broadcasted earlier than usual today: 4:20 A.M. I shall not complain, Lord. That will be the last one I hear at that hour, since today is the final day of our trip.

Our first stop was at Yad Vashem, the Holocaust Memorial built in memory of the six million Jews who were slaughtered in World War II. Lord, I don't even know what to say about this. Right now at this moment, I have no words... only feelings of anger and bitterness, and I'm doing my best to eliminate them.

When we entered the Historical Museum, I went down for the count. There were many displays of actual documents from Hitler's "final solution to the Jewish problem," German government publications matter-of-factly reporting their extermination goals, and wall after wall of enormously disturbing photographs of the unthinkable massacre. There are some horrifying images that I can't get out of my mind, Lord. I find myself asking, "Why? Why? WHY did this happen?" But I know I must wait for You to explain it — along with the 9/11 whys — on the day we finally meet.

David had briefed our group beforehand, then he told us to quietly walk through the museum at our own pace. But inside it was crowded with several large tour groups, and they were far from quiet. Many insensitive people were laughing and talking with each other in complete disrespect. I know You've heard this from me before, Lord. I complained about that same oblivious attitude at the Church of the Condemnation and on the Via Dolorosa. Maybe it's me. Maybe I'm oversensitive and I expect too much from people. Maybe this is another test to see how well I can just tune out the distractions.

But no, Lord, this time is different. How can I just tune out a person who walks through a Holocaust Museum chatting on his cell phone? How can I simply ignore a group of giggling young girls as they lean against a display case of nerve gas containers? The noise and the laughter diminish the impact of the memorial and dishonor the victims. The indifference of the people was almost as alarming as the event of the Holocaust itself.

It was an emotionally difficult experience, Lord, but it also heightened my appreciation of Israel and its people. I have spent the last two weeks learning about the ancient history of the Jews, and today I absorbed the awful reality of their recent history. Yad Vashem cemented my support of their determination to keep this land that You promised to them. Humanity is capable of committing the most heinous crimes... but the rebirth of Israel reminds me that with You there is hope after despair. With You there is victory after defeat. With You there is resurrection after death.

And Lord, *if* I ever visit the new 9/11 memorial in New York, and *if* I hear someone playing GameBoy while I'm reflecting on the inscription of Jim's name, please help me to exercise restraint — lest there be another incident at Ground Zero. Amen.

✦ ✦ ✦

Lord, the very last site we visited before we head back to New Jersey tonight was Calvary and the Garden Tomb. What more perfect way to end our trip than to see where You died and rose again?

We came to the hill called Golgotha (which is Place of the Skull in Scripture), which has the appearance of a skull within the rock formation... it's the location believed to be Calvary. Nearby at the foot of Calvary is a tranquil garden and an empty tomb — called the Garden Tomb — and it dates back to Your time. No one is really sure whether this was actually Your tomb or not — only You know for sure — and it's probably better that it remains a mystery, lest we idolize the spot instead of You.

We walked through the beautiful, quiet, lush garden. We looked up to the flat, green top of Calvary and imagined three crosses there. Everyone was quiet… everyone was praying as we stood in a solemn line of people waiting to enter the tomb. When it was my turn, I entered and knelt down. All I could say was, "Thank You, Lord… thank You… thank You." I didn't know what else to say, and I still don't have the words to express how I feel. Please just search my heart and mind and know how grateful I am, because "thank you" doesn't even come close…

+ + +

After dinner, David (our Jewish tour guide) told us that he bought Benny (our Jewish bus driver) a New Testament Bible today… because Benny was "interested in knowing more." Wow, that's huge, Lord.

We drove to the airport — begrudgingly — and said our poignant farewells to Benny and David… we miss them already… went through more heavy-duty security, interrogation, and meticulous luggage inspection… then boarded the plane for our long trip home.

I was in the center seat; Mike had the aisle; and a tall, thin man wearing a *kippah* over his graying hair squeezed his way around us and sat next to me in the window seat. He buckled his seatbelt, leaned against the window, and was sound asleep before the plane even took off. He woke up five hours later when the meal was being served. I noticed that he was frantically searching for something, and I asked him if everything was okay. "My kippah, it must have fallen off… I can't find it." (A *kippah*, or *yarmulke*, is the skullcap that Orthodox Jewish men must wear on the crown of their heads. In Jewish law, a man's head must always be covered, especially while eating and praying.) I helped him search the floor, the seat, the blanket — to no avail.

"It couldn't have gone far," I said. "You had it on while you were sleeping. It has to be around here someplace." I could sense he was distressed, not only because he could not eat without it, but because he had lost something precious. We kept searching.

Then Mike remembered that he had bought a kippah a few days earlier, and he had packed it in his carryon luggage. I'm not exactly sure *why* Mike bought a kippah, and I had discouraged him from wearing it since he's not Jewish and has no use for one; plus I feared it might be offensive or construed as mockery. But You knew it would come in handy, Lord, and You put it on Mike's heart to buy it and pack it in his carryon. Mike said to the man, "I have one. It's brand new — would you like to use it?"

The man's face lit up. "Really? Do you? Yes, thank you! That would be great!"

So Mike fished the kippah out of his luggage and gave it to the relieved man, who looked as if he had been handed a million dollars, promptly secured it to his head, and we all started eating.

"Thank you *so* much. Are you Jewish?" he asked as he popped the lid off his salad.

Mike and I both chuckled. "No... we're Christians."

"Wow! Really? So... how is it that you had..." he smiled and made a gesture, pointing to the kippah.

Mike glanced at me and gave me the "see-I-told-you" look. "I just wanted one. I'm in love with this country and its people, and I wanted to bring something home to show my Sunday school class."

And that was the beginning of an intriguing, enlightening, and unforgettable conversation that lasted the remainder of the flight. His name is Perry. He lives with his wife and grown children in Tel Aviv. He makes his living as a computer software engineer. He was flying alone to New York for a friend's wedding. He considers himself a modern Orthodox Jew.

The three of us talked freely about our religious differences. There was no criticism, no awkwardness, no threat of persecution, no fear of being ridiculed, no pressure to defend our beliefs. It was a deep, friendly, theological discussion based on sincere curiosity and the desire to understand each other's faith. Perry had many questions for us, and we had many questions for him. He wanted to know why we believe that You are the Messiah. We wanted to know why he rejected You. We openly discussed our spiritual similarities and differences, and we shared verses from the Old Testament and the Psalms. Mike and I listened intently to the testimony of his Jewish heritage, and we admired the passion in his voice. He listened intently to our conviction of Christ as our Lord and Savior, and he was fascinated by our confidence. We talked about the current events in Israel, the politics of Zionism, and the threats of terrorism. We asked if it disturbed him that a mosque stands on top of the Temple Mount and that many Israeli cities are now controlled by Palestinians. He said that some Jews believe these compromises are necessary to maintain an acceptable degree of peace among the Jews and Arabs.

We told Perry about all the places we had visited in the past two weeks. He beamed with pride and joy at our excitement. He told us about several places we wanted to visit but had been unable to fit into the schedule, "for *when* you come back next time..." he stated with confidence. He asked us if we had visited Yad Vashem, the Holocaust Memorial.

"Yes, as a matter of fact we were there earlier today."

His expression became solemn as he told us about his own family's tragedy. "My grandparents were killed. All my aunts and uncles. The only one who survived was my father, and he just died last year."

My heart felt like it had been pierced. The horrifying images on the walls of the Holocaust Museum came rushing back into my mind along with the contempt... the sorrow... the sick feeling in the pit of my stomach. Perry spoke calmly about the loss of his family, but the deep, painful scars were evident in his voice. I admired his strength and courage to talk about it without showing vengeance or hatred. He had every justified reason to be bitter with the world, but his warmth, kindness, and sensitivity prevailed. Lord, I couldn't help but think that Perry was a wonderful example of Romans 12:21... "Do not be overcome by evil, but overcome evil with good."

Then Perry changed the subject and asked Mike what he did for a living. Mike explained that he was a carpenter. Perry joked and said, "Doesn't have anything to do with that guy, Joseph, does it?"

We laughed as they talked about cabinets and materials and the differences between the construction of homes in Israel and the States. Mike got up to stretch and take a walk around the plane, and Perry asked me what I did for a living. "It depends on what day of the week it is," I said, referring to the pharmacy, my writing, and my speaking ministry. Then I told him about Jim.

Perry's eyes filled with tears, and he swallowed hard and took a deep breath. He looked down at his lap, unable to speak. Finally, he quietly said, "I'm so sorry. I never met anyone who lost someone on September 11th."

Tears were rolling down my face, and I put my hand on his arm. "I'm sorry too. I never met anyone who lost someone in the Holocaust."

And we sat on that plane, crying together, an older Jewish man and a middle-aged Christian woman. Two complete strangers with different backgrounds, different generations, different religious beliefs, different cultures, and different lifestyles… yet those drastic differences between us were bridged by the tragic events in our lives.

When the flight landed in Newark, Mike and I didn't want to get off the plane. Not only did it force us to confront the reality that our vacation was over, but it meant we'd have to say goodbye to Perry. We wanted to fly another eleven-and-a-half hours back to Israel with him, knowing that we wouldn't run out of things to talk about. As we were leaving our seats, Celeste (a member of our group who sat in the row behind us) discovered Perry's missing kippah on the floor under his seat. The mystery was solved *after* the friendships were formed.

Lord, only You could have pulled this one off. You brought the three of us together on that flight, and our seats were by divine assignment. Through the use of a simple kippah, You broke the barriers of contrast and made strangers into friends. Lord, Mike and I will never forget Perry for as long as we live. He is a sensitive man with a heart for God. We pray for Your blessing upon him and his family, and we pray that they will come to know You, their true Messiah. Please keep them safe in their troubled surroundings; and if it is Your will, perhaps our paths will meet again. His presence on that flight was the perfect ending to a perfect trip, Lord… and I have no doubt that You planned it that way.

Friday, March 18, 2005

Lord, thank You for bringing me home safely… and for the most amazing trip I've ever taken in my life. I have never experienced such a broad spectrum of emotions in such a short period of time. One minute, my heart was about to burst with joy and love as I immersed myself in the indescribable beauty of Your land; the next minute, I was startled by the armed soldier who waved a wand from my head to my toes before I entered a store in Tiberias. One minute, I'm laughing so hard at Sue as she sat on the 2000-year-old excavated public "toilets" in Beit She'an; the next minute I'm crying with gratitude for the blessing of time spent with You alone on the Sea of Galilee. One minute, I stand in adoration of the fact that You lived here, walked here, preached here, performed miracles here... next, I'm in tears because You died for me here... then I'm in a speechless state of awe and reverence because You rose from the dead here... then I can barely contain my excitement to know that one day You'll return here. Sometimes, the anticipation of an event is greater than the event itself, and we end up being disappointed by our high expectations. That was absolutely *not* the case here, Lord. I had hoped and dreamed and prayed for a good trip, and You gave us "exceedingly abundantly above all" that we could ever ask or imagine. I am so grateful for Your tender mercies, Lord.

And I thank You for everyone in our group — our fellowship was so enriching and I know You brought us all together by Your grace and love. I thank You for Pastor Fisher and his priceless wisdom and insight on the Holy Land. I thank You for David and Benny and their enthusiasm for making this an unforgettable experience for all of us. I thank You for the time we spent with Perry in good company and great conversation. I thank You for my three special speaking opportunities: addressing the group in Nazareth, reading the Sermon on the Mount of Beatitudes, and reading John 18 at the Church of the Condemnation. I thank You for good weather... for good health... for safe travels...and for countless cherished memories...

Lord, my experience in the Holy Land has certainly given the

Bible a whole new spin! And I have a much greater appreciation for the people of Israel and for our freedoms here in America. I have learned so much on this trip to the Holy Land... I know I am a different person for having been there, and I pray that I may return again one day.

Shokran, Yasoúo. (Arabic)

Toda, Yeshua. (Hebrew)

Thank You, Jesus... for making me teachable.

Overlooking Jerusalem from
the Mount of Olives

Acknowledgments

With deep love and everlasting gratitude, I thank my dearest family — Mom, Dad, Maria, Tom, Kevin, Brian, Anthony, Carla, and Tarah. I am so blessed to be born into a family who loves and serves the Lord, and I thank Him for that gift every day. Thank you for introducing me to God and for helping me grow closer to Him. You will never know how much your constant love, support, and encouragement mean to me... and I thank you for walking beside me on this amazing journey of my life.

To my dear friends — how I wish I could acknowledge each one of you by name... but alas, there is not enough space in the galaxy. I am so grateful for your patience and understanding, especially when my days get so hectic that I don't even return your e-mails and phone calls right away! (I'm sorry!) You share my laughter, my tears, my joy, and many cherished memories... and I thank God for the blessing of our friendship.

To my church family — thank you for showing me God's love, comfort, and wisdom... and for guiding my path and strengthening my walk with the Lord. Thank you for our fellowship together as students, soldiers, and servants for Christ. Thank you for teaching and maintaining sound doctrine, for being good examples to follow, and for being steadfast prayer warriors!

To "Team Teachable" — David, Brian, Nina, Mike, Heather, Scott, Sharon C. and Sharon F. — thank you for giving me the inspiration, courage, and confidence to pursue a career in writing and speaking. It has come to fruition only because you all responded to the Holy Spirit working in your heart, and for that I am truly grateful. Thank you for putting forth so much time, effort, and energy on these projects and for making *Tempered* and *Teachable* become a reality!

To the countless people who have been with me on this journey since 9/11 — perhaps we met briefly, or perhaps we've never met at all — yet your kindness, compassion, and generosity have touched me deeply, and I thank you with all my heart.

To the One seated on the Throne, to Whom this book and my life is dedicated — thank You, Lord, for opening my heart and my mind to a new and deeper understanding of Your love, Your grace, Your power, Your majesty, and Your victory. All I can say is, "Wow..."

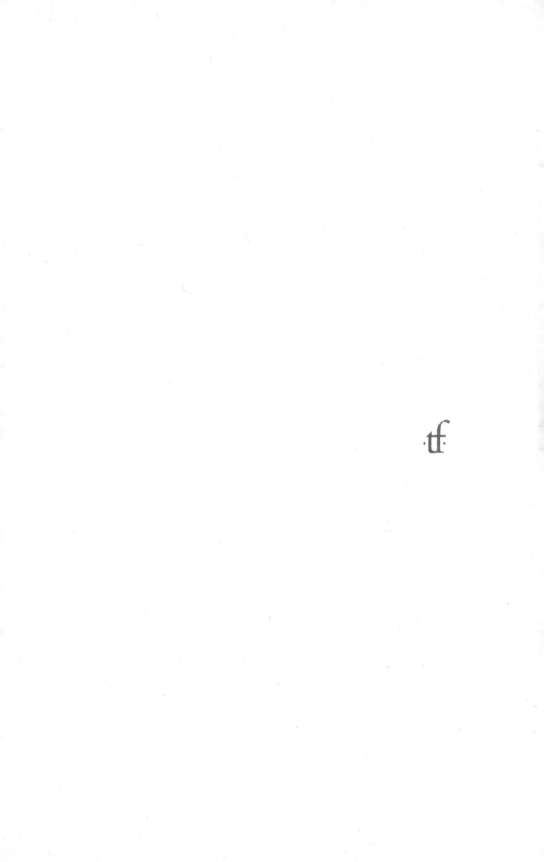

About the Author

Jennifer Sands is a New Jersey native, where she graduated from Ocean County College with a degree in business. She subsequently earned her pharmacy degree from Philadelphia College of Pharmacy and is a member of Christian Pharmacists Fellowship International and Rho Chi Society, the National Honorary Pharmaceutical Organization.

Jennifer continues to work part-time as a pharmacist; however, the main focus of her work is now writing and speaking to local, national, and international audiences on overcoming life's struggles through faith.

A Tempered Faith

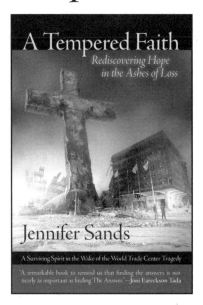

A *Tempered Faith* is Jennifer Sands' gripping, firsthand account of a young widow's questions, doubts, and desperate search for answers in the wake of her husband's murder. It is the emotionally raw journal of a battle to find footholds of faith in the midst of sorrow and spiritual darkness. Most of all, it is a joyful confirmation that what the Bible says is true: God is in control, He is listening, and He does love and care for us... even when the earthly evidence suggests otherwise.

US $17.95
ISBN-10: 0-9770794-2-2

Available to the booktrade through all major wholesalers.
Distributed to the trade through STL/Faithworks.
For more information, visit: **www.jennifersands.com**